FIT TO ENDURE
the Fire

Unless otherwise indicated, Scripture quotations are taken from the King James Version (KJV), New International Version (NIV), and Amplified Version. All rights reserved.

Copyright 2012 by Darryl L. Hill

ISBN 978-1-937095-66-6 (pbk.)
Printed in the United States of America 2012—First Edition
Cover design by Ana Saunders of Es3lla Designs

Published by Godzchild Publications
a division of Godzchild, Inc.
22 Halleck St., Newark, NJ 07104
www.godzchildproductions.net

Library of Congress Cataloging-in-Publications Data
FIT TO ENDURE THE FIRE/DARRYL L. HILL

1.Hill, Darryl L. 2. Personal Growth 3. Spiritual Growth
4. Christianity

All rights reserved. Except as permitted under the U.S. Copyright Act of 1976, this publication shall not be broadcast, rewritten, distributed, or transmitted, electronically or copied, in any form, or stored in a database or retrieval system, without prior written permission from the author.

Table of Contents

ACKNOWLEDGEMENTS
FOREWORD

PREFACE..III

1. BUILT TO LAST.......................................1
2. HELP! MY FAITH IS WAVERING...................11
3. YOU CAN'T AVOID THE TEST!...................23
4. CAN YOU HANDLE THE MEAT?...................35
5. THE ENEMY CHECKLIST...........................47
6. SO YOU THINK YOU WANT MY ANOINTING?...................................61
7. I AM ON YOUR SIDE...............................75
8. NOTHING GROWS WITHOUT A PROCESS......................................89
9. ONLY GOD GETS THE GLORY!...................99

10. BUILDING ON A SOLID FOUNDATION..................115

11. YOU ARE FIT!..................127

12. A REWARD WITH MY NAME ON IT.........139

ABOUT THE AUTHOR

This Book is dedicated to the memory of
Robert E. Carter
Savion Johnson
Jermaine "Blacko" Williams
and
To a special friend, Tanita Robinson, your endurance through the Fire inspired me to finish this book. Your friendship, grace and selflessness will always be remembered.

Acknowledgements

First and Foremost, I would like to thank God for His divine mercy and infinite grace shown to me during the process of creating this book. I am extremely grateful for the labor and faith of everyone involved in the production of this writing. Without the love and support from my family, friends, and colleagues, this book would have never come to fruition.

A special thanks to my devoted wife, Samantha; for your consistency and strength throughout all of my endeavors. What can I say about my two beautiful daughters, De'ajah and Samara; for their endless patience and understanding for what I am called to do; daddy loves you!

Thank you to my mother, Catherine Hill; for your resilience and undenying care for me. Thank God He's chosen you to nurture the gifts that are inside of me. To my father, Wallace Mitchell, I honor you. To my siblings, D'Ann, Donald, Deitra, Daniel and Dawn; our experiences together have made me the man I am today; I truly love all of you guys. To the greatest church on this side of heaven, Powerful Praise Tabernacle; you are the fruit of my labor and the expression of the assignment that has been given to me. I appreciate your sacrifices!

With gratitude, thanks to Dr. Jamal Bryant for encouraging me to take another step in the development of this project as well as your contribution in writing the foreword for my first book; truly invaluable. Thank you to Godzchild publishing, for your hard work and understanding of my vision for this book. Thank you to Bishop David G. Evans and Abundant Harvest Fellowship for your support; my home away from home! To all the people that I haven't mentioned by name, that worked behind the scenes, your unwavering commitment and love towards me will never be forgotten.

It is my prayer that this book encourages every reader to endure the fire and finish the race off strong.

Foreword

TRANSCENDENCE OF THE PHOENIX

The phoenix is a mythical sacred flaming bird that can be found in the mythologies of the Persians, Greeks, Romans, Japanese, Egyptians, and Chinese. This mythical firebird with a 500 to 1000 year life-cycle will literally make an offering of itself. Near the end of its life, it builds itself a nest of twigs that then ignites; both nest and bird burn fiercely and are reduced to ashes, from which a new, young phoenix or phoenix egg arises, reborn anew to live again. Its ability to be reborn from its own ashes implies a symbol of rebirth, restoration, and renewal. The whole point of the phoenix metaphor is that the apparent ending is where the story begins. At the heart of every version of the Phoenix legend, is a demand to risk in the present, to fly to the future, to accept the reality that your finest moments are always before you. Adversity is an opportunity of dying into a new birth.

Phil Stutz and Barry Michels argue in their book, The Tools, "Adversity is the weight against which you develop your inner strength." No doubt, within every individual lies a hidden inner strength that cannot be discovered unless one pushes oneself through adversity. Frederic Nietzsche, a daring thinker of the late 19th century, squeezed the concept into an aphorism when he declared, "whatever doesn't kill you will make you stronger!"

While Nietzsche was the first philosopher to project the positive value in adversity, his life as a hermit deeply diminishes practicality out of philosophy. The flaw in this logic attempts to relay adversity as the cause that makes one stronger. However, it doesn't! The reality is that inner strength comes only to those who move forward in the face of adversity.

Viktor Frankl, author of Man's Search for Meaning, has perhaps taught as many people how to survive adversity as any single author ever will. Frankl's experience as a concentration camp prisoner in Germany in World War II is chilling and inspiring. Virtually his entire family was murdered in the Holocaust. Still, Frankl found a way to sustain a sense of personal meaning in life and not be destroyed by the events that happened to him. Everything precious including our dignity can be taken from us, Frankl wrote, but the one thing that cannot be taken away is our power to choose what attitude we will take toward the events that have happened. He had a fantasy in his mind that gave him the strength not to choose suicide. He imagined himself, after the warm standing before a classroom of students. In his fantasy, he was teaching students about the meaning of adversity. There comes a time when it is essential to let a problem, a wound, a source of pain, be released because in the words of Viktor Frankl, "what is to give light must endure burning." It must endure burning, and it must come through both complete and new. Sometimes it demands that you suffer with dignity, sacrifice convenience, and never abandon your assignment. This provokes inner greatness while contending with outer grief. The worship of outer success breeds a selfish fixation on achieving our own goals. However, inner greatness develops when life makes your goals impossible. You are forced to reconcile your plans with what life has planned for you. Your accomplishment is not what you are now but what got you to where you are now!

I am fascinated by Pastor Darryl Hill's provocative book that comes more from experience, equipped with personal precepts and processes on how to endure adversity. This book is a proven practicum that will empower you to spend less time deliberating on whys and instead, focus on how and what to do after adversity. Beyond the hurts of life, there is always the transcendence of the phoenix; there is always a silver lining on every dark cloud and a bright light at the end of every tunnel. This masterpiece is a testament that proves being with God doesn't stop one from having tribulation; however it protects one in tribulation. Every fire will not break and destroy you but build and purify you. Life is much more than the sum of its pain. This is a must read!

Rev. Dr. Jamal H. Bryant
Bestselling Author, *World War Me, Vol. I & II.*

Preface

We live in a world where we can have anything we desire in an instant. We can order movies on demand, we can enjoy drive-thru meals, and nowadays, they even make minute-microwaveable rice! Everything is immediate. Everything happens so fast. It has gotten to the point that we no longer value hard work or teach our youth the importance of a dedicated work ethic. Ethics? Dedication? Those words and actions have become an endangered species. We would rather play the lottery to "win big in an instant" than to work hard until retirement. Our young people strive to become NBA players or a celebrity so that everything in life can be handed to them overnight, but the reality is, it doesn't happen that way. Life isn't a lottery and success doesn't typically happen overnight. In fact, the majority of people in the world aren't one-hit wonders; they are lifetime workers. They are people who earned their keep, and most likely, they started from the bottom and built their way to the top.

It's an ironic world in which we live.

Our mentors and idols are reality stars and glamour dolls; but interestingly enough, the life we see on television is furthest away from the reality we know and experience on a day-to-day basis. It's a dangerous season and an interesting time. People of faith must be careful not to conform to the trappings of this world. We know it has become a problem when Christians, from all across the country, are signing up for eHarmony and Christian Mingle instead of waiting on God to be connected to their mate. Contrary to what these sites would have you believe, God doesn't need the assistance of a social network to connect you with your spouse. We run to conferences for a quick prophecy, instead of falling to our knees to be in communion with God. Saints, we have got to slow down and incline our ear unto the Lord. Everybody wants their Internet to download at warp speed. We can't even wait for Netflix in the mail anymore; we want to watch it right NOW! Even our 'supposed' leisure time is planned, concise and rushed. We are a very impatient and privileged civilization— even down to our meals, which can be prepared almost faster than the speed of light.

So, why would our faith be any different? "*Wait* on the Lord" is the sermon we hear the least, but let's be honest: who has time for that? I think the concepts and spiritual disciplines of fasting, praying and waiting are an obsolete notion, just like our lack of perseverance. I believe people do not like to take their time to obtain things. We don't enjoy going through certain obstacles because we know that we'll end up quitting in the middle of the process.

When you were a child, I'm sure you read the book "The Little Engine That Could." The gist of the story was simple. In short, the engine thought he could get over the hill and he kept on trying. He didn't stop working until he succeeded. He didn't get distracted by what the other trains were doing. He realized his challenge, and focused on the prize. Our Christian walk is identical to the story of that locomotive. It's not when and why you start that matters; it's how you finish. It matters less if you finish faster than the person you are racing next to, your pace and assignment may require more planning and work, so just focus on finishing your specific task!

Finishing is everything. God doesn't start a thing and leave it incomplete. When Christ came down to take on the penalty of our sins, He cried out three words while hanging there lifelessly on the cross, "It is finished." Jesus finished what He started, so why have his followers left so much work undone?

We as believers have to garner up enough spiritual gumption to take on everything that life has to offer, and succeed. No matter how bad the medicine tastes, we have to learn how to swallow it and proceed with our mission; the first and most important mission being to spread the gospel of Christ Jesus.

All of us reading this book are similar to *The Little Engine That Could*, but our fate is different. We have a sure fire guarantee that what we receive at the end of the race is actually greater than the race itself. We have to be certain that we understand that our test lies in the race itself, how hard we train, how often we train, and the amount of effort we put forth during this training. Knowing these essential components will make all of the difference in the world.

It's Time to Pass the Trial Period

As a religious leader, it concerns me greatly when I see tenacious newcomers fizzle out in the very beginning of a race. This is very similar to people's New Year's Resolutions or going on a diet. People begin with the right attitude and drive, but quickly lose interest and energy. The reason for this is varied and could differ depending on the individual, but for the majority of us who are reading this book, we are the only subjects holding us back from doing the will of God. *Fit to Endure the Fire* was written to encourage and uplift the committed believer. Each chapter is inspired by a familiar passage taken from the book of 1 Corinthians. I'd like you to take a moment to read each verse closely, so that your eyes of understanding will be opened as we discuss this layered topic in the coming chapters.

---

1 Corinthians 3:1-15

And I, brethren, could not speak unto you as unto spiritual, but as unto carnal, even as unto babes in Christ. I have fed you with milk, and not with meat: for hitherto ye were not able to bear it, neither yet now are ye able. For ye are yet carnal: for whereas there is among you envying, and strife, and divisions, are ye not carnal, and walk as men? For while one saith, I am of Paul; and another, I am of Apollos; are ye not carnal? Who then is Paul, and who is Apollos, but ministers by whom ye believed, even as the Lord gave to every man? I have planted, Apollos watered; but God gave the increase. So then neither is he that planteth anything, neither he that watereth; but God that giveth the increase. Now he that planteth and he that watereth are one: and every man shall receive his own reward according to his own labour. For we are labourers together with God: ye are God's husbandry, ye are God's building. According to the grace of God which is given unto me, as a wise masterbuilder, I have laid the foundation, and another buildeth thereon. But let every man take heed how he buildeth hereupon. For other foundation can no man lay than that is laid, which is Jesus Christ. Now if any man build upon this foundation gold, silver, precious stones, wood, hay, stubble; Every man's work shall be made manifest: for the day shall declare it, because it shall be revealed by fire; and the fire shall try every man's work of what sort it is. If any man's work abide which he hath built thereupon, he shall receive a reward. If any man's work shall be burned, he shall suffer loss: but he himself shall be saved; yet so as by fire.

My prayer is that each chapter in this book will free your faith, and help you to endure the trials you are currently facing. You may see your trials as a heavy weight, but God sees them as a light affliction. You may think you need millions of dollars, but God has already made provision for every project He has commissioned you to begin. One spiritual mandate always leads to another river

> **ONE SPIRITUAL MANDATE ALWAYS LEADS TO ANOTHER RIVER OF PROVISION.**

of provision. So, as you read, imagine this book as the vacation you've been longing for. See it as the rest stop that runners go to for a minute in order to grab a cup of water before they have to run again. See yourself at the pit stop of life, in your NASCAR vehicle, and receive the fuel God is pouring into your spiritual tank. If you're not into sports or sprinting, then see this book as the intermission or recess period where the actors take a quick break and then jump back into the task at hand. Wherever you are in the race, I'm writing to assure you that you will finish the course. God doesn't waste his time on tentative people, so you were already fit before the foundations of the world!

Fit to Endure the Fire is God cheering us on... now it's time for you to believe in yourself again!

Chapter 1

Built to Last

1 Corinthians 3:1
And I, brethren, could not speak unto you as unto spiritual, but as unto carnal, even as unto babes in Christ.

I am a fan of contact sports—you know, like basketball, football and boxing. There's something about the impact of trained athletes that excites me. I've always been partial to these kinds of sports, but baseball and golf...really don't do it for me.

Anyway, there was a major fight airing and I was really excited to watch. One of my favorite fighters, Floyd Mayweather, was fighting Ricky Hatton. So I got together with a few deacons from the church and we all eagerly watched in anticipation. The big question of the night was obvious, "who was going to win?" These professional boxers weren't fighting for fun. They were fighting because they wanted to be crowned the champion. There was a lot of money at stake, so their loss meant everything! It was the difference between filet mignon for dinner or McDonald's; a house in the Hamptons or a house on Martin Luther King Blvd. Not to mention, there were "outside people" who were betting on them and their loyal fans whom they didn't want to disappoint.

So here we are—watching and focused; anticipating the winner that I wanted to take home the gold. In the beginning of the fight, it appeared as though Ricky Hatton was going to win because he was working double-time. We noticed how much energy he was exerting, and he was throwing out punches like ushers give out programs on Sunday morning! I'm telling you, Ricky Hatton threw what seemed like 50 to 100 punches in one round. But Floyd, on the other hand, didn't move as quickly. Instead, he paced himself the entire time. For the duration of the fight, he kept it slow and steady, slow and steady; and at the end of the fight, he hit Ricky with *one lightning bolt of a punch*. That one punch laid Hatton out. Next thing you know, he was on the canvas! Ten rounds of energy and quick moving, but one punch was all it took to knock the opponent out.

> **WHEN YOU STUDY MORE THAN YOU SHOW OFF, YOU TEND NOT TO WASTE TIME ON FUTILE THINGS.**

It was at this point that I realized something. This fight had nothing to do with technical skill. It didn't matter how much power or strength the boxer had. It had more to do with endurance. It had more to do with one's ability to sustain the fight long enough to find their opponent's weakness. It had to do with study and not skill; reservation and not exasperation. That's what endurance is. When you study more than you show off, you tend not to waste time on futile things. When you reserve your energy for the moments when it matters, then you are not exasperated and exhausted at the end of the night.

Endurance. It is the God-given ability to keep on going when everyone else around you quits. It's the gift of consistency. You may not run as fast as the lead runner, and you may not move as quickly as the people around you, but endurance pays off in the end. Why? Because while everyone else is busy catching their breath, your easy gliding pace will guide you right into the finish line.

FINISH STRONG

I've come to realize that God is not looking for people who are good at starting fast. He's looking for servants who will finish strong. It matters not if you are in the lead during the first few rounds. If you're on the floor at the end of the night, then all of your training and energy has been spent in vain. All of the tears you've cried and all of the sleepless nights have nevertheless left you defeated. And let's face it—who wants to be defeated? Who wants to leave the old nature of sin, find Christ, get sanctified, change our entire wardrobe, change the friends we're connected to, change the places we go—and still end up in the loser's circle? Who wants to tithe every week, and come to church thirty times a month just to end up in a posture of defeat? If you're anything like me, I want to win every race I run. I want to triumph over every enemy that's tried to keep me down. My life is too valuable to waste it on practice games. I don't have time for games. I don't have time for practice relationships. If you don't love me, then leave me alone. If after two weeks I see that you don't qualify, I will dismiss you from my life before I put up with anything substandard.

That's why my friends have changed. That's why I find myself alone more than I find myself in a crowd. Why? Because I want God more than I want my own satisfaction. I've got a race to win and a God to glorify. I've given up too much, I've labored for far too long, and after sacrificing this much, I'm expecting a crown in the end!!!

If this is you, then the key to your victory is not in your energy; it's in your endurance. The key to your triumph is not in your talent; it's in the time you put in after the crowd goes to sleep.

Stop for a moment and take inventory of your life.

Can you last through the whole fight?
Are you a finisher?
Do you start multiple projects?
Do you leave more work undone than complete?

Look at your home.

How much unresolved stuff have you left on the couch on your way to church?
When you change clothes, do you throw your clothes every-

where and leave piles of laundry for others to clean up?

Do you wash dishes after a meal or do the dishes in the sink reflect the issues you let pile up over time?

Do you use church as an intermission from real life, only to avoid the people whom God is calling you to talk to on a weekly basis?

Who are you and how do you behave on your job or in school? Is your supervisor constantly reprimanding you for showing up late and leaving early? Are you committed to anything? Are you the student whom others can trust to get the job done, or do you send emails the night before with a lame excuse about the dog eating up your homework? How many relatives have to pass away for you to see that time waits for no one? How many people have to get sick for you to finish your degree and become who God called you to be? Aren't you tired of losing easy races? Aren't you tired of your excuses? I know my excuses are surely tired of me!

NO TIME FOR EXCUSES

Here's the blunt truth. People of endurance have no time for excuses. They see life differently. And the fact of the matter is, the time has come for all of us to drop our excuses and build ourselves up in the faith. The expiration date for your excuses have come and gone. It's now time for you to release them and do what needs to be done. I believe that is what the Lord is ultimately saying to each of us who are saved. It is not about how rapid you perform your task for God or how powerful you may be when you are standing before people in public, but the real question is - *can you last throughout the duration of your tenure?* What is your consistent momentum like? How long can you keep up the pace? Read this verse again with a new understanding:

1 Corinthians 3:1
And I, brethren, could not speak unto you as unto spiritual, but as unto carnal, even as unto babes in Christ.

That's the first nugget of truth in 1 Corinthians 3:1. When Paul says "I could not speak to you as unto spiritual but unto carnal," what he is really saying is, "I need to give you the basics before I give you the complicated." Some of us are so addicted to the spiritual that we are humanly shallow. We need to learn what God is saying through an example like boxing before we can master the mystery of godliness through spiritual warfare. Stop trying to bite off more than you can chew!

The boxer wasted all of his energy on the front end of the race, and had nothing left for the most important rounds. He's like so many of us who spend all of our money as soon as we get our check, only to end up broke and borrowing money at the end of the month because we don't know how to balance our checkbook. If you're going to be a man or woman of endurance, you've got to learn how to balance your life. You should never give so much of yourself in the beginning of a relationship that there's nothing new to discover about you in the latter years. You should never give so much of your time in the beginning of your job that people develop expectations of you that you can't sustain later on. Balance says, "I will not choose work over worship if I can help it." Why? Because work is putting money in your pocket, but worship is breathing life into your spirit. Both are important, but my spirit is far more important than the money I have in the bank.

> **WORK IS PUTTING MONEY IN YOUR POCKET, BUT WORSHIP IS BREATHING LIFE INTO YOUR SPIRIT.**

Think about it.

What good would it profit a rich man to have a broken spirit—you'll always be leaking out on someone; always feeling like you never have enough; always feeling like you have to prove something to someone. Why? Because your endurance levels are low. You are off balance. You need to hear me in this chapter, or nothing else will connect to your fitness through the fire. *Lasting can only happen if you learn how to pace yourself.* You've got to develop a stride that works for you and maximize on your greatest strengths. The Bible clearly states in Ecclesiastes 9:11, that the race is not to the swift, nor the battle to the strong, neither yet bread to the wise, nor yet riches to men of understanding, nor yet favour to men of skill. In the end you've got to endure. Don't become the new member who enters with zeal, tenacity, and strength, but in three weeks, you are nowhere to be found. Pace yourself and ask the Lord to perfect your spirit of endurance. Once your spirit of endurance has been perfected, it is very unlikely that you will not finish the race, or faint before you finish. That's the greatest benefit of having perfected endurance. You may not finish first; you may not finish when others expect you to; and sometimes, you won't even finish when you expect yourself to; but the fact of the matter is, you will finish and not faint. Why? Simply because the Lord has granted you to the ability to endure until the end.

Chapter 2

Help! My Faith Is Wavering

1 Corinthians 3:2

I have fed you with milk, and not with meat: for hitherto ye were not able to bear it, neither yet now are ye able.

Have you ever been aboard a ship and you felt that you were going to sink? Usually people who go on cruises for the first time are extremely nervous. Why? Because they don't have control over how they will arrive from one place to the next. They are completely in the hands of another person. And I don't know about you, but anytime I find myself in an uncomfortable position, it can be a nerve-wracking experience. It's unsettling, I'm uncomfortable, and I pray in tongues a lot more when my life is in someone else's hands!

If you are not a sailor, you don't have any experience with boats. So that puts your life in the custody of someone else who is either more or less efficient than you. It's no different than riding a plane. The turbulence on a plane will cause your body to react. As you're sitting in that small chair next to people you don't even know, your stomach is doing jumping jacks and your mind is thinking a million thoughts-- *"What if this is my last time on Earth?", "What if I never see the break of day again? Who haven't I forgiven? What did I forget to do at home? Is there anyone else I should say "I love you" to?*

I am sure you will agree: life has a way of shaking you up with turbulent moments. When someone passes away or if you lose something special, it somehow reminds you of your immortality. It confirms something in us that we already know—we will not be here forever. Life is but a blade of grass--it's here today and gone tomorrow. But if we learn to appreciate those turbulent moments in the midst of our storms, then we can make it through anything. Faith is realized during turbulent situations. The moment you see an opportunity for God in your life, that is also the moment when something has caused or incited turbulence. *Be Honest.* Most times, it's in the bad days that God's hand is most visible. It's in the bad seasons that my image and reputation take a back seat, and I begin to reach out for God's help. The bad days are signs that the grace of God covers us even when we are not at our best; even when we're not doing our work to the best our ability; even when we don't get the "A" on the test, and despite the fact that we just got fired from our job. It's in moments like these when we need to endure the fire and seek God for an answer.

> **IT'S IN THE BAD DAYS THAT GOD'S HAND IS MOST VISIBLE.**

In my experience as a pastor, I have learned how fickle some people really are. Some people, not you of course—but *other* people reading this book have developed a horrible pattern. They opt to hang their faith up on a shelf whenever the sun is shining and they totally ignore God as long as everything goes okay. But the moment their spiritual plane experiences turbulence, they will run to the church and bombard the pastor until he lays hands. Yes, we all do it...don't we? We run to the church mothers to pray. We start coming back to church for 5 weeks, and then when our lights come back on, we are nowhere to be found!

Let me help you here.

Faith isn't a tool that we put into practice only when we face bad days. Faith is just as important on a good day as it is on a bad day. It's an everyday life choice; a gift that God has given us, and we should treat it as such!

FAITH IS JUST AS IMPORTANT ON A GOOD DAY AS IT IS ON A BAD DAY.

FAITH IS ESSENTIAL

In this chapter, we must talk about faith. Faith is an essential ingredient that most people do not include in life's recipe. It's imperative that we do not leave the house without it! Wherever you go, your faith should be right with you. Think of faith as one of your favorite accessories- that one accessory that you wear with every outfit even if it doesn't match with anything that you are wearing on that day. That's how you should view faith. You cannot endure the fire without faith. There should never be a time when you are caught in life's activities without faith. You need faith in everything that you do. You need faith in every place that you go. Plain and simple-- you cannot succeed at anything if you are devoid of faith.

———————— **Hebrews 11:6** ————————
And without faith it is impossible to please God, because anyone who comes to him must believe that he exists and that he rewards those who earnestly seek him.

Scripture tells us that without faith it is impossible to please God. Many preachers I know have the right hoop. Many singers I know have all of the riffs and runs down pat. There are even those of us who show up on time for every church meeting, and others of us who never miss a bible study. I'm sure you know at least one church mother who arrives at worship on Sunday morning before the deacon even gets there to unlock the church doors—and yet, without faith, it is impossible to please God. The reason God is not pleased is because we are present, but faith is absent. We are excited, but faith has exited the building. The lesson here is this—you can do everything the way it should be done, but if you are doing it without faith, God is not pleased.

FAITH IS NOT SIMPLY AN IDEA OR A POPULAR CHURCH WORD; IT IS THE SOLID ANCHOR THAT GROUNDS EVERYTHING THAT YOU DO.

Faith is not simply an idea or a popular church word; it

is the solid anchor that grounds everything that you do. If you don't have faith, you don't have an anchor; which means you don't have anything to secure you when needed. This is why so many people never endure the fire.

Let me ask you a question. Are you so busy trying to serve God that you are missing God? Are you so busy trying to do everything and be everything to everyone that you haven't paused to see what your anchor is grounded in? If your anchor is grounded in man, you will always be tossed to and fro. Why? Because men change like the weather. But if your anchor is grounded in God, you will have sustainable faith; you will have endurable faith, and you will have long-lasting faith.

I want you to graduate to a place where your faith doesn't waiver. What does one do when everything around you starts to go crazy? In this particular scripture, Paul is talking to a church at Corinth- a specific church whose faith is wavering. These people put more emphasis in their pride, and in their own knowledge than in the wisdom of God. I want to encourage you to grow in the wisdom of God. No matter how many degrees you have, no matter how much money you have in the bank, no matter how many credentials you have accumulated, you have got to invest in the wisdom of God. The wisdom of God will save you time. The wisdom of God will save you money. The wisdom of God will give you new ideas, new dreams, and new vision. Without the wisdom of God, you only have your own might and your own strength. But when you operate in the wisdom of God, you literally move from faith to faith.

So, Paul is addressing the church in Corinth and realizes that these are a people of many personalities, who have come together to build a strong city. This city is based on commerce and trade, which tells me that this is not a broke area. Rather, this area has been built on good finances and on a solid economy. Most times, many people who have faith in themselves are successful people and they make a living off what they do. But when you hit the bottom of the barrel and you lose everything, what are you going to stand on?

The people in this text prided themselves on their knowledge and riches, but they didn't have a sure anchor. They were viewed as influential but they didn't have an anchor. They had great economic status but they didn't have an anchor. They could talk circles around presidents, kings, and queens, but they didn't have an anchor. My friends, it is so important that you identify Christ as the only anchor in your life. If you don't, you can't endure. If you don't, you won't last. When was the last time you sat down to investigate how strong your anchor was? How strong is your prayer life? How strong is your devotional time?

How do I know when a member is anchored in faith? It's simple. If the pastor offends or rebukes them, they still show up to church. They don't catch a temper tantrum and storm out like most anchor-less people do. If you are not anchored in faith, you will run the moment someone hurts your feelings. You will withdraw membership from the church because the choir director didn't give you a solo. Too many people are not anchored, and for that reason, their faith is fickle. But God is looking for people of God who are anchored in the faith; people who won't wait for the good days to come in order to love God, but they will joyfully bless the Lord at all times. It is not enough to just be anointed. You must also be anchored.

> **IT IS NOT ENOUGH TO JUST BE ANOINTED. YOU MUST ALSO BE ANCHORED.**

GET AWAY FROM DOUBLE-MINDED PEOPLE

James 1:1-8

James, a servant of God and of the Lord Jesus Christ, To the twelve tribes scattered among the nations: Greetings. Consider it pure joy, my brothers and sisters, whenever you face trials of many kinds, because you know that the testing of your faith produces perseverance. Let perseverance finish its work so that you may be mature and complete, not lacking anything. If any of you lacks wisdom, you should ask God, who gives generously to all without finding fault, and it will be given to you. 6 But when you ask, you must believe and not doubt, because the one who doubts is like a wave of the sea, blown and tossed by the wind. 7 That person should not expect to receive anything from the Lord. 8 Such a person is double-minded and unstable in all they do.

Here in this text, James tells us that a double minded man is one who is blown and tossed by the wind. Not only are the people in Corinth double-minded, but they are surrounded by double-minded people. Everywhere they go, they see a reflection of their dysfunction. Listen Carefully. I encourage you to rid yourself of double-minded people. Double- minded people are like germs. If you come into contact with them, you will eventually become sick and start behaving the way they do. Trust me. If you knew anything about double-minded people, you would make it a priority not to be around them at all! Double-minded people will make you doubt the word of God. Double-minded people will make you turn around and go back to the place from which God has already delivered you. Double-minded people are delirious and distracted. They make up things that aren't true. Double-minded people are perilous people. They will praise you in your face and then talk about you behind your back. One week they will sing "Hosanna in the highest" and the next week they will be screaming "Crucify him!"

If you are trying to live a balanced life and if you want to endure the fight, then I beg of you to flee from every double-minded person that is around you. Anyone who ALWAYS has to take a second and third guess when making simple decisions, or anyone who is extremely indecisive and can't decide what they want to do in life, falls in the category of a double-minded person. Don't move from this chapter until you are certain about your friends and your faith. You've got to figure it out now. Consider the emphasis scripture of this chapter once more.

1 Corinthians 3:2
I have fed you with milk, and not with meat: for hitherto ye were not able to bear it, neither yet now are ye able.

With this scripture in mind, the big question is: are you still on milk or are you eating meat? A child cannot handle the food that their parents eat. A baby can only handle milk because their digestive system hasn't fully developed. But if you can handle meat, that means you are anchored; that means you are solid; that means you are stable and confident in the God that you serve. Sure, you need the water of the word to wash down your food, but if you can handle meat, then you can also handle rejection, abandonment, and humiliation. You won't run and leave when everyone else runs and leaves. You will ignore gossipers and people that mean you no good--that's how you know if you are on meat versus milk. People of meat are people of anchored faith- their faith isn't contingent upon their circumstances or the things that are taking place around them. Their faith is connected to the God that they serve.

Now that you have an idea of what the prerequisites are to be a person of meat and a person of anchored faith, there are just a few questions that you should pause and ask yourself. Are you reading the word daily? Are you putting fuel in the fire? Are you filling up your spiritual tank the way that you should? If you answered yes to these questions, then you are ready for Chapter 3.

Chapter 3

You Cannot Avoid the Test

1 Peter 4:12

Friends, when life gets really difficult, don't jump to the conclusion that God isn't on the job. Instead, be glad that you are in the very thick of what Christ experienced. This is a spiritual refining process, with glory just around the corner.

The lesson of this chapter is very, very simple: YOU CANNOT AVOID THE TEST. If you are fit to endure the fiery trials of life, then there is no way you will be able to skip the famous time called "testing time." I believe the reason we try to skip this season in our lives is because we have become spoiled by God's favor. We have become spoiled by God's provision. What do I mean by that? *I'm so glad you asked.* In my humble opinion, it appears that when we call upon the Lord and He answers us, we then create a pattern of expectation, thinking that God will do the same thing today that He did for us yesterday. But what you must come to understand about faith is that there will come a day when God will not speak or move the way He did before. God spoke to Moses through a

> **THERE WILL COME A DAY WHEN GOD WILL NOT SPEAK OR MOVE THE WAY HE DID BEFORE.**

dark cloud one day, and God spoke through a burning bush on another day. We grow from faith to faith. We elevate from glory to glory. You may not feel the difference, but the fact is, you are stronger now than you were before. And if you are stronger, then God will change the rules to elevate your faith in Him. In this season, you no longer need a teacher. Now, you need a mentor. The differences between a teacher and a mentor are vast in comparison. A teacher will talk you through the rules step by step, but a mentor will be silent during the test. A mentor will not talk you through every chapter, but they will walk you through the instructions and necessities to complete said task without holding your hand.

The mature Christian will accept God as mentor--the God who will be there for you even when it's dark; the God who will sit back and allow you to fall because in the end, He knows that every fall will teach you something valuable about life. God is the kind of mentor who will never let you skip a class and will expect you to pass every test. God as teacher will nurture us, burp us, baby us, bridle us, and help us in the elementary stages of life. So here lies the question: Do you want to be taught or do you want to be mentored? If you're still on milk, then you're accustomed to the teaching posture of God. This chapter, however, focuses on those who want to be mentored and will therefore say "yes" to the test.

Like every graduate program, there is no way that you can matriculate into the next field of learning until you have passed some fundamental, standardized tests. Tests are given for the purposes of building you. Tests are administered in order to help you evaluate your strength. You know how strong a structure is built based upon what you put on top of it. So, the stand that your television sits on is one with a strong foundation. If it wasn't, then you wouldn't place your valuable television on top of it, in fear that it would be too weak to hold the television. The same is true in the kingdom of God as it pertains to the tests and trials of life. If God doesn't put anything on top of your structure, how will He know what you can handle? How will he know what you are made of? If God doesn't send the issues of life your way, or if God never tries you with any number of circumstances, then how will He know what your faith can handle? Don't always blame the devil for what God might be doing to test you. The Bible clearly tells us to expect certain things when they happen to us.

1 Peter 4:12-13

Beloved, think it not strange concerning the fiery trial which is to try you, as though some strange thing happened unto you: But rejoice inasmuch as you participate in the sufferings of Christ, so that you may be overjoyed when his glory is revealed.

These verses are clear. The trials of God come to strengthen us. When God tests us, He's coming to elevate our minds, transform our habits, and grow us up. But the question is, how high do you want to go? How much do you want to grow?

You Can Only Withdraw What You Deposit

I have discovered an interesting fact about life. Life can be lived on various levels. If you want to go higher, then you have to be willing to accept the next test. If you don't desire a greater level in life, then you can cruise on the same level for the rest of your days. In fact, there are really only two types of people- people who are fit for the challenge and people who would rather sit on the sidelines. There are those who will apply for the promotion and then there are those who will stay at the same work level for years, and complain that they are not making enough money. There are those who change the system, and those who are too afraid to do anything different.

When you think about your track record, how would you describe yourself? Are you fit for challenges or are you quick to settle? If you are fit for the challenge then you are also prepared for the challenge. You've already studied for the test. You aren't waiting to be surprised by life's unexpected events. Being prepared means that you are ready and ahead of the game. As a matter of fact, it means you are one step above your opponents. Everything you do is advanced. And, the same is true for how you view the blessings of God. If you want to receive, you've got to have an advanced praise; you've got to have an advanced understanding; and you've got to put in some advance work. Your advance work is what will advance you in the Kingdom. Gone are the days of the welfare mentality. You will only withdraw what you deposit! God will pour out based on what you have put in! Therefore, if you do not put in, God cannot pour out. *Isn't that simple?* It seems so very easy to understand, but I bet you'll be surprised to discover how many people struggle to comprehend this Galatians 6:7 principle. On this journey, we all must learn to deposit that which we expect to withdraw. Certainly, you can't visit the bank and withdraw money that you never put in. Your spiritual bank account is no different. If you deposit unrestricted worship, then you will withdraw unmerited favor. If you deposit time in the Word, then you will withdraw revelation from the Word. No deposit. No withdrawal... it really can't get any simpler than that!

LIFE'S CHALLENGES

So, again, I ask; what kind of person are you? Are you the person who is willing to accept the difficulties of life, knowing that these challenges will make you stronger? Or are you the kind of person that will sit there blaming everyone else for the things that you did not achieve? I don't know about you, but I cannot sit around people who blame other people for too long. Why? Because their toxic blame game spirit will seep into the pores of my potential, draining my purpose and the very life God has called me to live. If we live life blaming everyone else, then who will we blame when we stand before the Father on judgment day? Who will we blame on that final day of Judgment, when the pearly gates swing open and the Lord pronounces, "Well Done.." or "Depart from me?"

If I become accustomed to living life while blaming everyone else, then I will not be prepared for God's response in heaven. God isn't interested in excuses. No matter the challenge, God is looking for a people who are ready to match each challenge with faith in action. Do not forget where God has brought you from. Fundamentally, the way we grow our faith is by remembering what God brought us through before. The way we pass God's tests is to remember how God prepared us for the pop quizzes before the final exam! Focus on what you know. You know who you are! You are an heir and joint heir with Christ. You have been born into the Kingdom of God. You already know that there is therefore now no condemnation for those who walk in the Lord. And you know that Jesus has died for every one of your sins. Therefore, you have direct access to the Father through Jesus. What you already know is that you are more than a conqueror. What you already know is that God majors in your minor; He always makes a way for you. So if he did it before, He will do again! As you embark on this new journey, and as you prepare for this new test, you have got to remember what you already know!

> **THE WAY WE GROW OUR FAITH IS BY REMEMBERING WHAT GOD BROUGHT US THROUGH BEFORE.**

UNDERSTANDING THE TESTS

Understand this: everything you are going through today is preparation for your blessing around the corner tomorrow. There are life-giving ideas that God has to press out of you. The only way He can get it out of you is to test you. The only way He can evaluate how well you are doing is to test you. Tests are not coming to annihilate you and weaken you. No real teacher will administer a test hoping their students will fail. Rather, tests are given for the purpose of you realizing what gifts you already have within you. You need the test so you can congratulate yourself for growing past some things. The same way we weigh ourselves after working hard in the gym, the spiritual test is an invisible scale that helps you to see the pounds you dropped since the last time you measured your sanctification weight. The heavier God's weight of glory sits on you, the lighter you become. The better you are. The freer you get!

> **UNDERSTAND THAT GOD INCREASES US BY FIRST DECREASING US.**

God never gives a lazy student a promotion. God never wastes tests on people who do not want to grow. So, if you are experiencing multiple tests, you are getting ready to receive multiple blessings. God prepares those of us who are ready for more through the spiritual act of a test. A test will refine you. And if you understand the refiner's fire, you understand that God increases us by first decreasing us. God promotes us by first demoting us! God stretches us by first shrinking us, God expands us by first putting us on reserve, and then He makes our name great by causing us to serve in low places as a prerequisite to the big blessing around the corner.

Sister, brother, your greatest blessing is right around the corner. I know this test might mean that you will have to preach at a homeless shelter for a year before you ever preach at an international conference. But this test is all about humility. This test is about strengthening the minister within. God wants to know if you will be able to handle the platform if He puts you somewhere that challenges your character. If God is working on your patience, then you may have to work in a daycare for 5 years just so that you can master nurturing the innocent children in the world. How you treat the babies in the daycare will hint at how you treat babes in Christ.

All of these are tests that God uses to refine, grow, cultivate, and build us. You can't avoid them; you can't grow around them… so you might as well just take them! If you go to the gym, you understand that the trainer has already sized you up and he already knows what you are capable of doing. God is our life coach. His job is not to keep you at the level you came in at. His job is to press you to the point of non-ability, to the point where you stop believing in yourself and you allow God to take over. When you allow God to take over, your muscles are stretched, your wisdom increases, your possibilities expand, and later, you discover you are able to do far more than you could ever do in your own strength. And trust me, once you catch revelation of what the test signifies and what it has done for you, you will no longer beg the teacher to make the work less difficult; you will no longer go to the trainer asking him to remove pounds from the bench press; because you recognize how much more you can handle. You recognize the power that is working within you. And most importantly, you recognize that Greater is the Teacher who is giving the test, than the student who is taking it!

> **GREATER IS THE TEACHER WHO IS GIVING THE TEST, THAN THE STUDENT WHO IS TAKING IT!**

Chapter 4

Can You Handle the Meat?

John 8:32

And ye shall know the truth, and the truth shall make you free.

In 1992, a very famous movie hit theaters all over the world; one which I'm sure we are all familiar with, titled, "A Few Good Men." In this popular movie, there were two key actors- Tom Cruise and Jack Nicholson. Recall the scene where Jack Nicholson is sitting in the courtroom. Tom Cruise is trying to force him to answer a few uncomfortable questions. And Tom Cruise nudges Jack to answer him truthfully, but Jack opens up his mouth in vehement exhilaration and yells, "YOU can't handle the truth!" YOU CANT HANDLE THE TRUTH!

What a powerful climax to any movie scene. These words have become a popular mantra in American culture--YOU CAN'T HANDLE THE TRUTH--but, the interesting fact plaguing many readers today is that this statement is true. Most of us only know a few people who can, honestly, handle the truth. *Think about it.* Why do you think people walk around living a lie all of their lives? Why do people clothe themselves in fashionable garb or in name brand clothing that is luxurious to the eye but too expensive for their pockets? Why do we live above our means, cover our faces with makeup, or hide behind toupees? We do all of this, in part, because we don't know how to reconcile with the truth. We don't know how to *live with* the truth. We say to people in church that we are having a great day, but secretly, we are in the midst of trying times. In some cases, our current situation is so bad that we have no idea where our next meal is going to come from. We have no clue how our rent will be paid or how we will survive the next day, but we are having a great day? *Come on. Let's tell the truth.*

When Jack Nicholson made the statement "you can't handle the truth," he was addressing Tom Cruise. But there is a deeper question that I would like to pose to you. My question is, can you handle the *meat*? You may be wondering what I mean by that, so permit me to remind you of some important points from the previous chapter. Remember, Paul is writing the church in Corinth, and is explaining the difference between babes in Christ (those who drink milk) and mature believers (those who consume meat). Let's be clear though, because I do not want you to misinterpret the definition of meat. Members of Christ's body who can handle the meat are mature in Christ. "Milk" Christianity, however, does not necessarily imply immaturity; it could just mean elementary. In other words, you are on a certain level in God that requires a little more attentiveness and pruning. If you are in the milk stage of your Christian walk with God, there are certain responsibilities that God will not bestow upon you. It's not because you aren't qualified or smart enough. It's just that God wants to mold you and make you before He can trust you with certain assignments and tasks.

Think of it this way. If you enter a job at an entry level position, the chances of you receiving the master keys to the office are highly unlikely. Why? Because you are a new employee. You are just "learning the ropes." However, once you have put in ample time and earned seniority on the job, then you will gain the benefits that "newcomers" aren't afforded. The same is true with God. God waits until we have put in the time before He entrusts us with the key. To be on milk means that you have been granted access into the ways of God. To be on milk means that God is holding you and cradling you just as a mom holds her infant child. To be on milk means that you are learning the ways of God, so that God might fill you, use you, and elevate you at the appointed time. On the contrary, if you can handle the meat, then you've also endured some tough experiences in the faith. It means that you are not wet behind the ears and you have been tried in multiple fires! Your faith does not waver because you are grounded in God.

WHO ARE YOU LIVING TO PLEASE?

Galatians 1:10
Am I now trying to win the approval of human beings, or of God? Or am I trying to please people? If I were still trying to please people, I would not be a servant of Christ.

People of meat desire to please God and God alone. They love people, but they don't live for the approval of mankind. Ultimately, they live for the approval of God. On the other hand, people of milk may find themselves looking for a man to validate their identity, not realizing that God wants them to look beyond man's finite thoughts in order to embrace the infinite revelation of God. Your focus and motivation are two determining factors when discerning what you can and cannot handle. Here is why: if you are a minister whose main focus is to be validated, accepted, or approved by others, then we know how much you can handle. If you need a crowd of people to fill the pews whenever you minister, then this clearly insinuates that you are a person of milk. On the other hand, if God is the center of your focus, and you are absolutely engulfed in offering up an acceptable sacrifice in His sight, then you are without question a person of meat.

My question to you again is, *can you handle the meat?* Can you handle the tests that God is baking up just for you? Can you handle the trials that come with the territory of being a sold out disciple of Jesus Christ? The worst thing you could ever do is enter into an opportunity, a classroom, or a relationship unprepared. Take a moment to assess how much you can handle. The meat of the matter is very simple. It all boils down to suffering. When you are able to endure suffering, then that tells me whether or not you can handle meat. Some people do not want to deal with suffering so they attempt to run away from it at all costs. The truth is, if you are ready for meat, then you are ready to suffer. The Bible declares this truth in at least three different passages.

In 2 Timothy 2:12, Paul says: "If we suffer, we shall also reign with him: if we deny him, he also will deny us." In this passage, Paul makes it clear---if we want to reign with Christ, then we must first suffer with Him. Furthermore, this passage shows us the truth behind real ministry. Before there can ever be a period of reigning, there must first be a period of suffering. Notice, the scripture doesn't say, "if you give a sizable offering, then you will reign with Christ." It doesn't say, "if you sing on the choir, then you will reign with Christ." It doesn't even say, "after you become the most anointed preacher in all of the world, then you will reign with Christ." The Scriptures don't say that. Instead, it argues that your level of elevation is contingent upon your level of suffering intake, which consequently comes as a result of your "yes" to God.

> **YOUR LEVEL OF ELEVATION IS CONTINGENT UPON YOUR LEVEL OF SUFFERING INTAKE.**

It is imperative for you to understand that your "yes" to God will cost you. It may cost you friends. It may cost you popularity. It may cost you your convenience, but the only way to be a true disciple is to suffer through your unequivocal "yes." Suffering for God is surrendering to God without asking God "why me?" Suffering for God means that you commit to obeying God, even when you cannot see the fruit of your obedience. To suffer for God is to endure fierce ridicule and marginalization, and still show up to church on Sunday without a beam of anger or jealousy in your eye. To suffer is to be done wrong, to be criticized, and to be gossiped about; yet still determined that nothing will separate you from the love of Jesus Christ.

> **PREPARE FOR THE BRAND OF SUFFERING THAT COMES PACKAGED IN A PROBLEM BUT DRIVES US DIRECTLY TO THE SOLUTION: JESUS CHRIST.**

The second scripture is a popular one, but many readers tend to overlook one small detail written in *Galatians 5:22*: "*But the fruit of the Spirit is love, joy, peace, **longsuffering**, gentleness, goodness, faith.*" Among the recipe of Spirit-led attributes mentioned in this passage, the seed that is most neglected in the body of Christ is longsuffering. Notice: it doesn't say that suffering will be temporal, transient, or seasonal. It says that you will suffer long. In other words, you've got to prepare to go through some things for a long time. Prepare to be frustrated. Prepare to be torn down or talked about. Prepare to be disappointed. Prepare to be bombarded. Prepare for the brand of suffering that comes packaged in a problem but drives us directly to the Solution: Jesus Christ.

When you are ready to graduate from milk to meat, you are prepared for a long battle. You are prepared for a long trial. You are prepared to be in school for five to seven years until you earn that doctorate. You are prepared to remain in that marriage even after the "love butterflies" go away. This kind of maturity doesn't happen overnight. One thing you must know about suffering is that it does not have an appointed time of duration. Suffering will last for as long as God allows, until its purpose is fulfilled in your life. You must endure hardness as a soldier in the army of the Lord over time. God blesses the believer in increments. God never gives or entrusts big blessings or big vision to people who have a microwavable mentality. Longsuffering is not like a bag of popcorn that you pop in the microwave and then after two minutes, it's done. That is not how it works. Longsuffering strengthens your endurance; and God is looking for his children to endure the fire, stick it out, and remain steadfast. These are God's requirements before He entrusts us with the next move of God.

> **GOD NEVER GIVES OR ENTRUSTS BIG BLESSINGS OR BIG VISION TO PEOPLE WHO HAVE A MICROWAVABLE MENTALITY.**

In the third scripture, Philippians 1:21, Paul says: *"For to me to live is Christ, and to die is gain."* His philosophy on life is not quite like those preachers who preach convenient Christianity. His understanding of prosperity lies in the glory that comes with every lash to the body, and every slander to the soul. He says in no uncertain terms, *"I would rather die early than to live a moment in this world without Christ. If I am killed for the name of Christ, then so be it! Dying is better than having a penthouse suite overlooking the New York skyline. In my opinion, dying for Christ is living."* The saints of old knew what it meant to suffer for Christ, too. They used to sing a song during devotional that said, "If I die, let me die in the army of the Lord. If I die, let me die in the army." Why? Because these mature mothers could handle the meat. These saints had matured into a faith of unquestionable endurance. They were whipped by slave masters, and did not turn on God. Their bodies were taken advantage of, but they did not turn on God. They were often isolated and abandoned, but they did not turn on God. Instead, they looked to the hills from whence cometh their help! They turned to fasting and praying, to make sure their flesh lined up with the word of God. Their focus was fixed on Christ and Christ alone. The moment our mindset harmonizes with the mindset of our church mothers and our church fathers, we will become fully able to handle the meat.

SUFFERING MATTERS TO YOUR MAKER!

As you come into a fuller understanding of where you are in God's holy spectrum, keep in mind that suffering matters to God. Ministers, get ready to suffer! Evangelists, Prophets, Bishops, and Christian leaders, get ready to suffer. If you sense a call from the Lord, you are not just being called to ordained ministry; you are not just being called to wear nice robes; you are not just being called to write books. You are being called to handle the meat. You are being called to proclaim the truth. You are being called to suffer. In Luke 9:23, Jesus challenges us with these words: "if any man will come after me, let him first deny himself, take up his cross daily, and follow me." Self-denial is a form of suffering. Putting your agenda aside and carrying the weight of God's glory is a form of suffering. Whenever you decide to go to church instead of going to the club, that is suffering in action. Whenever you decide to remove yourself from toxic and unhealthy relationships so that you can live a holy lifestyle before God, that is suffering in action. Whenever you choose to accept a pay cut before compromising your Sabbath, then you have accepted the call to suffer for the name of Christ. These are all examples of suffering in action. These are all decisions that require you to deny yourself and deny your desires, so that your life will bring glory to God.

Pause for a moment and evaluate your life. Look deeply into every aspect of you. What is the status of your relationship with God? If God sat down to grade your commitment and willingness to suffer for His namesake, how would he grade you? Can God look at you and say, "this one can handle the meat"? Before turning the page, know that you can handle the truth. Know that you can handle the meat. But saying "yes" to the truth and saying "yes" to the meat means you will have to endure the hardships of life as a good and faithful soldier. In order to do this, you've got to say "yes" to it all –not just the good days but also the trying days; not just the days of mountainous overflow, but also the days of valley-like dependence on God. Simply put: more suffering produces more glory. If you can handle the meat, then you can handle the suffering. Why? because you know that on the other side of this, lies glory.

Chapter 5

The Enemy's Checklist

Matthew 5:44
But I say unto you, Love your enemies, bless them that curse you, do good to them that hate you, and pray for them which despitefully use you, and persecute you;

Do you remember the popular kids in your elementary school? Weren't they always dressed so nicely, or they were considered the "talk of the hallway," or they were sociable and funny, so everyone wanted to know them. If you were one of "those," then you couldn't possibly know what it was like to be the unpopular kid. You know the kind. They would sit in the front of the class. They were really shy, really weird, and really detached. During physical education or outside activities, nobody would pick the strange kid to play with. Nobody would ask them about their family life, and nobody---I mean nobody---would offer them a ride home after school. The outsiders were always treated differently than the insiders.

Well, like it or not, we still have an outsider/insider mentality in the church. It shouldn't be this way, especially considering that one of the key characteristics which distinguishes a Christian from a non-Christian, a believer from a non-believer, and a disciple from an atheist, is our ability to love. Love is what we do. Love is who we are. In fact, Christians from all around the world are known by how we love our friends (or the insiders), and also by how we love our enemies (or the outsiders). Love is the trademark of our faith. If you are going to grow in the faith, then you have to learn how to walk in love. When we come into the fullness of life, we realize that God is not preferential. In other words, He doesn't have insiders and outsiders. He doesn't rank us based on our eloquence, attractiveness, popularity, or intellect. In Christ, there is neither male nor female. Jesus loves us all; and He calls us to love all gradations of people. *Why? Because God is love.* Love is God. And love is not merely a quality or a characteristic that describes a part of God's makeup; love is the full embodiment and personification of all that God is. The true identity of Christ is love.

> **LOVE IS THE FULL EMBODIMENT AND PERSONIFICATION OF ALL THAT GOD IS.**

So, if love is who God is, and love is how God expects us to behave, then why do so many people hate on each other? Why is there an "inside clique" over here and an "outside clique" over there? How can we fully represent a God who loves all, and yet we harbor discrimination in our hearts against our brothers and sisters in Christ? We are not in elementary school anymore. It's time to grow up and love right. No matter where people have come from and no matter what they have been through, it is our

Christian obligation to love! Love is not a choice; it is a command! The day our churches will grow is the day when we finally learn how to love our enemies.

Believers of Christ, we are required and expected to operate in love. If we intend to be recognized as Jesus' disciples, then we have to take on the image of Christ and extend pure love, even to those who are undeserving of it. There is just no way you can live for Christ without loving those around you; be it your next door neighbor, the uncle that you'd rather not interact with, or the coworker that is trying to get you fired!

The call to love is the sequel to suffering. I know you want to be exalted in the spiritual realm, and I know you may desire to become a best selling author or musician, but what if God needs you to fill your love cup first? What if He needs you to pass a few more love tests? Before God promotes us, he needs to see how we treat the one who demoted us. He needs to evaluate our responses, especially when we speak to our spouse behind closed doors. He wants to see how we interact with our children. Are your kids a duty or a joy? Does your face light up when they walk in the room, or are you always sending them away to stay with some other "aunt" or "uncle" so that you can have a break? Do you send them to

> **BEFORE GOD PROMOTES US, HE NEEDS TO SEE HOW WE TREAT THE ONE WHO DEMOTED US.**

their room and ignore them all night? What do those closest to you think about your love behaviors? Our love capabilities will strengthen us if we allow them to; and our love tests will grow us up until we are sure that we are fit for the fire.

In the New Testament, the Scripture declares this truth: the greatest commandment is to love the Lord with all of thine heart, soul, and mind. In addition to this, the second commandment requires that we love our neighbors as ourselves (Matthew 22:37-38). Now, most times when we think of our neighbors, I'm sure most of us think of our *actual* neighbors; you know, those who live next door to us or those who live around the block or in our neighborhood. But that doesn't fully encapsulate the word "neighbor" in this text. The word "neighbor" here suggests everyone with whom we come into contact. The instruction is to love all, and the expectation is to love each person so profoundly, that a stranger never feels like a stranger; and a distant relative never feels like a distant relative. But our love becomes so genuine and pure that we make neighbors before we make friends. We make neighbors before we make business partners. We become helpers in the time cf need, because love is an action word. When we come to understand the heavy weight that love carries with it, we will bench press more in prayer and ask God to spot us along the way.

THE LOVEABLE VS. THE UNLOVEABLE

Before we go any further, I want you to pause for a moment. If I asked you to list 5 people in your life that you love without question, who would they be? And if I asked you to list 5 people who, in your mind, are "hard to love", who would they be? Do you see a different image of love when the unlovable faces pop up? Why or why not? Imagine if you could love the unlovable to the same degree, with the same smile, and the same enjoyment that you love the lovable.

All of us, whether we are ministers, pastors, or parishioners, have a few people in our phonebook whom we find hard to love. These are those who get limited time with us, who get limited attention from us, and limited conversation with us. These are those who see us walk all the way around the church to avoid them. You know, Sister Gossip or Brother Backbiter. When they show up, we go downstairs to use the bathroom five times. When they show up, we check out. But the truth is, God is testing our love capacity. The more you mature in Christ, the more you will be able to handle the fire.

Put those 5 people back on your mind, and commit to loving them more. Commit to listening to them with ears of concern and discernment. Don't be so quick to judge or to dismiss. Give them a little more time than you normally do. You might have to devise a plan. You may need to force yourself to "call him" or "call her" before you go to work. If love doesn't come naturally, then God is trying to work on that area in your life. I know it's challenging, but if you approach it with a determined mindset and a willing spirit, you will succeed at loving your enemies. Remember: the very thing that separates the mature Christian from the immature Christian is your ability to love, and to love means to freely display concern and compassion without reservation.

> **THE VERY THING THAT SEPARATES THE MATURE CHRISTIAN FROM THE IMMATURE CHRISTIAN IS YOUR ABILITY TO LOVE...**

It's easy to love someone when you feel as though they deserve it. It's even easier to love someone when your relationship with that person is going smoothly. However, the true test of love comes when you can love the one who least deserves it. When you can love the one who cheated on you; or walked out on you; or drug your name in the dirt; or stole your man! When you can love those enemies, you have just elevated into the same love Christ had for us when we cheated on Him, walked out on him, drug His name in the dirt, and stole His glory. Mature Christians live everyday with one goal in mind: love anyone; love everyone... especially those who are unlovable.

Identifying Your Enemies

The next question that needs to be answered is, *who are your enemies?* Who are your opponents? Who are those who mean you no good, if, in your mind, you don't see real enemies in your life? Well, firstly, if Jesus requires us to love our enemies, then we have to identify them. In fact, He tells us to bless those that curse us. So that means, by implication, before we can bless them, we have to figure out who they are! In order to do this, we have to sit down, break away from the crowd for a moment and pray. Ask the Lord to reveal who your enemies are. An enemy is not just someone that you don't like or someone that doesn't like you. An enemy is someone who distracts you from destiny. An enemy is someone who pulls you away from the will of God. An enemy is someone who is constantly deterring you from the path that God has placed you on. Enemies are not always dressed up in a red devil suit. Sometimes, your enemy could be the person who is closest to you, but is always giving you reasons NOT to complete what God has told you to complete. *Take Peter for instance.* Peter became an enemy of Christ, for just a moment; not because he had an argument with Jesus. Jesus was trying to prepare the disciples for his departure, and Peter tried to stop the process. Read the text for yourself:

Matthew 16:16-24

And Simon Peter answered and said, Thou art the Christ, the Son of the living God. And Jesus answered and said unto him, Blessed art thou, Simon Barjona: for flesh and blood hath not revealed it unto thee, but my Father which is in heaven. And I say also unto thee, That thou art Peter, and upon this rock I will build my church; and the gates of hell shall not prevail against it. And I will give unto thee the keys of the kingdom of heaven: and what-

soever thou shalt bind on earth shall be bound in heaven: and whatsoever thou shalt loose on earth shall be loosed in heaven. Then charged he his disciples that they should tell no man that he was Jesus the Christ. From that time forth began Jesus to shew unto his disciples, how that he must go unto Jerusalem, and suffer many things of the elders and chief priests and scribes, and be killed, and be raised again the third day. Then Peter took him, and began to rebuke him, saying, Be it far from thee, Lord: this shall not be unto thee. But he turned, and said unto Peter, Get thee behind me, Satan: thou art an offence unto me: for thou savourest not the things that be of God, but those that be of men. Then said Jesus unto his disciples, If any man will come after me, let him deny himself, and take up his cross, and follow me.

Isn't it interesting: the same Peter whom Jesus blessed is also the same Peter whom Jesus rebukes. Within minutes of each other, our greatest blessings can become our greatest burdens. Peter didn't fully understand what he was doing, but the enemy used him to try to stop the will of God from going forth. Peter wasn't focused on God, he was focused on his wants. The enemies of our lives could care less about what God said to you. They are concerned about what they can get from you. Their first question is, "what's in it for me," or "how can we straddle the fence and still get by?" Their greatest praise may tickle your ear, but if they do not line up with what God said, they are working against your future.

So Jesus turns and says to Peter, "Get behind me, Satan! You are a stumbling block to me; you do not have in mind the concerns of God, but merely human concerns." Jesus refers to Peter as Satan because he saw that his disciple was being used by the enemy. Whenever our focus is not on God, we become susceptible to the enemy's infiltration. Anytime your focus is not on the things of God, the devil sees that as a green light and will attempt to use you in whatever way he can. The enemy loves to prowl on those who are open and easily influenced. Fasting and praying are two spiritual tools that help to ensure that the door never opens up for the enemy to walk through. But Peter isn't done being used by the enemy. Later, when Jesus is washing the feet of his disciples, Peter tells Jesus not to wash his feet. Jesus then replies to Peter, "If I wash you not, you have no part with me" (John 13:8). In other words, stop trying to get in God's way by offering your opinion. Your greatest enemies are opinionated, forceful, and always disagreeing with someone. The best way to identify them is to listen. The enemy is speaking but you aren't listening. Who is the main person in the group that always has a problem with the plan? Who is the person presenting himself or herself as one way in front of certain people, but becomes another person when they are in front of other people? Who are the "friends" that never have your back, but always need a loan? Who are your "family members" that contribute in messing up the plans, but will not help you to clean your life back up? The point is, anytime someone comes against the will of God concerning you, they are undoubtedly your enemy. An enemy is someone who attempts to hinder you from where you are headed.

Once we understand who our enemies are, then we can love them the godly way. Jesus expects us to treat our enemies in the same manner as we treat our friends. He looks at the report cards of our lives to assess our love intake. Based on that grade, He makes a decision about our discipleship. If we are followers of Christ, then we have learned to pray for our enemies. But if we are crowd pleasers, then we are still holding grudges against those who have a grudge against us. Keep in mind: the enemies in our lives (and how we treat them) reveal to us if we are fit to endure the fire. Don't think for a second that loving your enemy is as easy as taking candy from a baby. Loving your enemies is by far one of the most challenging things to do, and quite honestly, it may be the very last thing you desire to do. However, it is imperative that you understand what Jesus Christ expects. The church at Corinth wanted to make up their own rules. But, if you want to be fit for the Master's use, then you've got to follow the Master's manual. The Master loved those who hated him! The Master didn't show partiality on the cross. He died for the very ones who were slashing him in the back. He calculated all of our sins, took them upon himself, and died while we were yet full of the sin. So, if Jesus could love imperfect people, why can't we?

> **IF YOU WANT TO BE FIT FOR THE MASTER'S USE, THEN YOU'VE GOT TO FOLLOW THE MASTER'S MANUAL.**

TO WHOM MUCH IS GIVEN

As you progress in your walk with Christ, you will find that the deeper you go in Him, the greater your enemies will increase. But don't allow this to deter you. Just remind yourself that Jesus endured it and empowered you to handle it. Thus, God will honor you for not walking away from Him even after others walk away from you. The fact that you have an opponent just means that you are living a life that is true and holy. If you do not have an opponent in your life, then I am forced to wonder if you are really a Christian at all. In this life we will suffer persecution, and if Jesus is the light of the world, then his followers ought to offend the darkness. If you are loveable and likeable to everyone, there is no possible way that you are living as a bold witness for Jesus Christ. When you are living life as a bold Christian, you frustrate sinners. You make the devil mad. When your enemies see you coming, they turn and go the other way; not because of anything you've done to them, but because of the stance you've taken for Christ. Don't be afraid of your enemies. Learn who they are, and then love them anyway!

THE ENEMY CHECKLIST

Take a look at this Enemy Checklist. Reviewing this will help you to assess where you are as it pertains to your enemies.

Enemy' Checklist
(Read each question attentively and provide a honest answer.)

- Do you know who your enemies are?
- Do you ignore their phone calls?
- Do you run away from them when you see them?
- Do you talk about your enemies behind their back?
- How well do you treat your enemies?
- When is the last time you prayed for them?
- Who do you struggle most to love?
- How often do you bless those that curse you?
- How often do you pray for those that gossip about you?

Now that you have reviewed the checklist and answered each question, you can now determine how much growing you have to do. Maturity can only be achieved after you realize and accept that there is a need for growth. You know what you need to do in order to improve, so do it! *Pray, confess, forgive, and be forgiven—love God and love your enemies. In that order.*

Chapter 6

So You Think You Want My Anointing?

Philippians 4:7-11

And the peace of God, which passeth all understanding, shall keep your hearts and minds through Christ Jesus. Finally, brethren, whatsoever things are true, whatsoever things are honest, whatsoever things are just, whatsoever things are pure, whatsoever things are lovely, whatsoever things are of good report; if there be any virtue, and if there be any praise, think on these things. Those things, which ye have both learned, and received, and heard, and seen in me, do: and the God of peace shall be with you. But I rejoiced in the Lord greatly, that now at the last your care of me hath flourished again; wherein ye were also careful, but ye lacked opportunity. Not that I speak in respect of want: for I have learned, in whatsoever state I am, therewith to be content.

Every year, large families come together during the summer to celebrate family reunions. Reunions, as you know, can be the best of times or the worst of times. Aunts and uncles are catching up with nieces and nephews. Children are being told "you look just like your mother," and parents are kicking their feet up by the pool to enjoy a few days off from work. These are the good times. But then there are times when family reunions aren't so great. The women are all in the kitchen and one wrong comment causes an explosion to break out. Big

Mama brings up memories about Aunt So-and-So, and Cousin So-and-So grabs a spoon and starts arguing. Not before long, the dinner that had been prepared for a loving family is being thrown around and the brawl has turned into a wrestling match.

It's one thing when friends have a disagreement. It's an entirely different thing when fights break out in the family.

We are a Faith Family

Whether you want to accept it or not, we are all brothers and sisters in the body of Christ. By the mere fact that we are connected to the Father through the atoning blood of Jesus Christ, means we must learn to love one another deeply. We are connected by a different kind of bloodline, and because of that, we must throw away all envy, jealousy and strife.

Every Sunday, we sit around the holy table to enjoy a little meal with the Lord. Every Sunday, we have a family reunion. Some Sundays are great days. The praise is high. The sermon is inspirational. The people you are sitting next to actually enjoy being next to you. But then there are other Sundays when we hear unnecessary bickering in the church. The alto wants to sing in the microphone instead of the soprano. The lady with a degree in Communications wants to read the announcements instead of the church mother who has been reading them for 55 years. The minister-in-training wants to turn in his resignation letter and start his own church. The young adult leaders start fighting about whether or not to invite Kierra Sheard or Mali Music, and before we know it, the family of faith has become a reality show of drama.

I told you in the last chapter: the day the church will grow is the moment we learn to love our enemies. But get this: our enemies should not be women and men who belong to the body of Christ. We shouldn't be fighting each other! Our enemies are those who are outside of the faith, and those that try to stop you from succeeding in the faith. In my opinion, faith fights are a waste of energy. When we participate in them, we use the strength that God has given us to combat the enemy to, instead, fight each other! So instead of positioning our weapons of warfare toward spiritual wickedness in high places, we start pointing our weapons toward one another! It's amazing to see how many people will sit in your pew and tear you down before they build you up. It's a sad thing to witness in church; women auditioning for the First Lady position, or men who only want to preach but never want to serve. Saints... when these symptoms show up in your church, there is a sickness going around that we haven't dealt with!

That sickness can best be defined as the "envy syndrome." You know the envy syndrome: when somebody wants what you have but they haven't been through what you've been through. **The envy syndrome.** When somebody would rather steal your job, your man, or your preaching style instead of developing their own. The envy syndrome is an epidemic problem that many churches face today. But this isn't a new issue. The church at Corinth faced it as well!

When Paul is writing to the church at Corinth, he is not just talking about mature Christians versus immature Christians. He's also taking out precious time to put out petty fires! For most of the chapter, he's speaking about the division that bleeds through healthy churches and tears down our walls of potential. He's talking about the strife and envy that come to poison and pollute God's people to the point of dysfunction. The worst kind of division is the kind that can be fixed in prayer, but is perpetuated by gossip. In other words, you can talk to God about your sister and God will work it out, but instead you talk about your sister to another sister, and plant seeds of discord among the faith family! Think about it. Both prayer and gossip require us to talk, but most people would prefer to talk to another human being, rather than speaking to the God who can solve the problem.

> **THE WORST KIND OF DIVISION IS THE KIND THAT CAN BE FIXED IN PRAYER, BUT IS PERPETUATED BY GOSSIP.**

Do not get caught up in the mousetrap of gossip. Those who do never make it out without being trapped themselves. Always remember that the very ones we talk about today will turn the table and spill our secrets tomorrow.

CHAPTER 6 *So You Think You Want My Anointing?* | 67

Can't We All Just Get Along?

It would be best if we all just got along and learned to support one another. But, of course, that isn't what happened at Corinth, and that is not what is happening in our churches. Nowadays, we see people vying for positions; auditioning for a spotlight like singers on *American Idol*; and none of this pleases God. Primarily, it displeases him because we offend the God who created us every time we try to be someone else. *That's right.* Every time you try to wear my outfit, squeeze into my armor, or preach like I do, you offend God. Why? *Because God made you unique.* If He wanted clones, He would've patterned us all the same. He would've copied our identities on the Xerox machine of heaven, and duplicated our purposes to do the same thing, to sound the same way, and to beat in sync with every other human being. But He didn't do that. God never intended us to be a household of clones. He made us to be unique and special in our own individuality; united by faith but not chained to it. The moment we try to be someone else, we say to God, "I'm not good enough as I am." The moment you chase after my dreams, you make it appear that God forgot to give you one. I cannot tell you how many people have longed to have the Sunday of my anointing, but if they knew the Friday persecution before Sunday came, they wouldn't want it so bad.

> **GOD NEVER INTENDED US TO BE A HOUSEHOLD OF CLONES.**

The Anointing is Costly

The more fires we endure, the greater our understanding of the *anointing* becomes. The anointing is a fancy word for "pain rerouted." The anointing is a spiritual muscle produced by pain. In order to get it, you've got to go through painful situations. Why? Because pain is nothing more than a catalyst of power. So, the reality is, more pain…more power. More power, more anointing. Less pain, less power and less anointing. If we realized how much pain was required for God to anoint certain individuals with the oil of purpose, we would stop envying other people's gifts and talents. Paul was anointed, but Paul was also persecuted, beaten, locked up (even though he was innocent), forced to starve and he wore the same clothes for weeks at a time—that's real pain! Job received double in the end, but before we get to the "happily ever after" episode, we can't forget that he lost everything. He lost his family, his cattle, his business; he lost it all. And when he needed strength, the only wife who survived told him to curse God and die. *That's real pain!*

You may wish you could call Isaac your son, but if you knew how many sleepless nights Sarah endured, waiting desperately for God to answer her prayer, you would leave Sarah alone and just serve God. I know you want to be the forerunner for Jesus like John the Baptist, but don't forget—John was beheaded for the sake of Christ. The pain of the anointing is a real-life experience. Every disciple will endure his or her own version of it.

So just because I look like one million dollars today doesn't mean I've never been homeless. You just entered my life at a chapter of provision, but you don't know the chapter called poverty that God brought me out of! You could never know the silent nights, the hollow days, the services I had to preach at where there were only a handful of sleepy listeners! These were the painful memories that produced a pure anointing.

> **YOU JUST ENTERED MY LIFE AT A CHAPTER OF PROVISION...**

DO YOU WANT THE GLITZ OR THE GOSPEL?

Those who envy your gifts are attracted to the glitz of ministry, not the gospel of Jesus Christ. The gospel of Christ includes death, burial, and resurrection. Until something within you has died, been buried, and resurrected, you are not ready to handle the call on my life. You couldn't handle my anointing if someone paid you to carry it for a day, so instead of envying my gift, cultivate the seeds that God has deposited in you. Every time you forsake your home to lust after someone else's, you leave your nest vacant for the enemy to come in and to destroy. Every time we meddle into someone else's family issues, we leave room for our family laundry to be aired out in unsafe places. How are you going to be fit to endure the fire if you're still trying to fit yourself into my anointing?

Accept Your Cup

When you look at me, you see a finished outlet that God plugs power into. But you don't know the months and years it took for God to gut me out, clean me up, and prepare me for use. Here's the lesson: Don't become so caught up in someone else's finished product that you neglect your beginning stages. You may one day obtain a public platform, but if God needs to work on your humility, you may have to start by cleaning the bathrooms. You may one day sing around the country and bless thousands, but if God needs to teach you more on the subject of surrender, then He may plant you in a storefront church with seventeen members and two broken microphones. God knows our end from the beginning. To lust after my anointing is to deny yours. You may not like this truth, but everyone can't be a singer. Everyone won't be a preacher, and everyone won't be anointed to shift atmospheres through an "earthquaking prayer" like Dr. Cindy Trimm. But God has made us different and diverse for His glory, not ours. Learn to accept your cup and stop trying to perform on my stage. The more you envy someone, the more pain you bring on yourself.

> **DON'T BECOME SO CAUGHT UP IN SOMEONE ELSE'S FINISHED PRODUCT THAT YOU NEGLECT YOUR BEGINNING STAGES.**

You can't look at a person who is mature in his or her gift and desire it. You don't know what they had to go through in order to receive it. The anointing over my life wasn't cheap. It was very expensive. I had to cry many tears for this anointing. I had to go through many things and I'm not talking about *before* church. I'm talking about things that went on right-in-the-church! I know you see me moving in ministry and I'm declaring and doing what God has called me to do, but you don't see the behind the scenes work that every servant of Christ must put in, in order to be used by God.

Practice Contentment

1 Timothy 6:6-10 (NIV)

But godliness with contentment is great gain. For we brought nothing into the world, and we can take nothing out of it. But if we have food and clothing, we will be content with that. Those who want to get rich fall into temptation and a trap and into many foolish and harmful desires that plunge people into ruin and destruction. For the love of money is a root of all kinds of evil. Some people, eager for money, have wandered from the faith and pierced themselves with many griefs.

The man who is content with himself, is blessed by God. The woman who doesn't envy things from the outside world, values her inner virtue. Endurance, suffering, handling the truth, and praying for your enemies are not the only signs of a mature

Christian. If you are fit to endure the fire, then you have also learned to be content. To be content means you will not complain if you do not receive the promotion. To be content means you will continue to praise God even if the spouse, children, two cars, pet, and mansion do not show up. The scripture declares that godliness with contentment is great gain. Paul learned in whatsoever state he found himself in, therewith to be content. If you can't learn contentment, then you aren't ready for commitment. Whenever you have to commit to something, there will always come a day when the work hours seem long; when the relationship goes dull; when the responsibilities become too heavy to carry, but contentment in Christ will help you to commit to others.

> IF YOU CAN'T LEARN CONTENTMENT, THEN YOU AREN'T READY FOR COMMITMENT.

How can I recognize a man or a woman ready for more responsibility? They do more behind closed doors and get paid the same amount. They have already walked into an elevated position but they haven't received the public crown. David was already king after Samuel anointed him, but he didn't take the public position immediately. He walked into his kingship but never changed clothes. A sign that you are content with what God has deposited inside of you, is when you can be all that God has made you, without making a public announcement to the world.

It's when you can give to the homeless without CNN following you with a news camera. It's when God can catch you in private being the same person that you are in public.

Paul reiterates, "there is still strife, envy and separatism among you." In other words, there are still situations and issues that are pulling you away from each other. There are still cliques amongst you. And when there is a lack of vision, people divide. Paul says, "I can still tell that you are immature because I left you in this same state and you have not grown. And now it's time for meat and you are still fighting one another." Paul couldn't have known that we would still be going through this today. But we are. The envy complex is a terrible disease. And no matter how bad you want Oprah Winfrey's money, President Obama's Success, Bill Gates' empire, Barbara Walters' popularity, or Warren Buffet's bank account, you can't have what they have because you haven't gone through what they've been through.

> **HE WALKED INTO HIS KINGSHIP BUT NEVER CHANGED CLOTHES.**

The money sounds great. The popularity is attractive. But if you haven't endured the tabloids, the criticism, the pundits, the negativity, the competition, the hardships, the difficult days, and the failures, then you have no idea what success really means. The same is true for the spiritual heavyweights you see in the world. I know Pastor Joel Osteen or Bishop Jakes have impacted the nation for the better. But it would do us all well to be content with the gifts God has given us.

I love you, but I don't want your anointing. Why? Because if I had it, I would also have to accept your fire. I would have to experience your rejection, your heartache, your unanswered prayers, your public humiliation, your negative press, your balancing act between family, faith, and fun, etc. We really don't know what others go through to get what they've got, so do yourself a favor, and stop lusting after that which you do not fully understand. Just practice contentment.

Chapter 7

I Am on Your Side

Matthew 18:20
For where two or three are gathered together in my name, there am I in the midst of them.

One of the greatest songs ever written was recorded a few years ago by a dear friend of mine, Bishop Hezekiah Walker. The lyrics in the song, *"I Need You to Survive,"* remind us of God's desire for unity. Ultimately, God wants His children to become support systems for one another. We are called to serve one another, love one another, and pray for one another. The lyrics in this song also remind us that God works best when two or three are gathered in His name. God never intended for the Body of Christ to be an isolated entity, separated from one another. I'm not certain when we picked up this idea of isolated Christianity: you know, the *Me, Myself, and I* complex. This mentality has divided the Lord's church into broken, fragmented pieces; but now is the time to declare, "I am not against you, I am on your side."

THE POWER OF TOGETHERNESS

Do you remember being in Preschool and having to put together those small puzzles? *You know the kind.* They were made up of various shapes and sizes. There were only about 8 or 10 pieces in the box, but it was difficult to complete the entire puzzle alone. Why? Because our cognitive abilities are not stretched to its fullest potential in isolation. The 3-year-old who succeeded at putting the puzzle pieces together, recognized a key that most of us do not have on our Christian key chain. The key to all success is unity. The key to all Kingdom building is tied to the proactive decision to come together. The moment we come together, we see another side of God. Where there is unity, there is strength. And where there is strength, there is a powerful manifestation. After we come together, we are able to unlock potential that we never knew we had.

> **OUR COGNITIVE ABILITIES ARE NOT STRETCHED TO ITS FULLEST POTENTIAL IN ISOLATION.**

Christians coming together cancels the plan of the enemy. John 10:10 reveals that the thief comes for three reasons: to kill, steal, and destroy. But did you know that he has a purpose attached to his mission? The enemy ultimately wants to steal our divine union with one another, destroy our families, steal our resources, and kill our trust. The enemy understands something that we have yet to fully realize. If he succeeds at turning Christians against another, he inevitably succeeds at disturbing the peace in the Kingdom. We have to make it a priority to ensure that the enemy's plots and schemes are never fulfilled because the truth of the matter is... Christians need one another to survive.

Take Inventory of Your Need for Others

Take a moment for internal introspection. Think back on the creation story in Genesis when the serpent tempts Eve. What does the enemy do to distract her? He comes in the form of a conversation with the intent of luring Eve away from the divine plan of God. From the time that Eve was deceived until now, the enemy has diligently sought to separate men from women, women from women, men from men, father from child, son from daughter, grandparent from grandchild, etc. He uses the small divisive seed of miscommunication to tear apart families. He specializes in dividing good things. He concentrates on tearing things apart. If you find yourself in the middle of a heated argument, you have two decisions: to instigate or to back away. The mature Christian will step back and ponder how much glory will be stolen from God if this conversation continues. The mature Christian will look at the situation, no matter how deep it has become, and take inventory of the bigger picture. The mature Christian will reconcile with the one who hurt them, as opposed to dismissing the very person who may have come into your life to promote you.

WE ALL NEED SOMEBODY!

Most times we don't realize it, but division, independence, and our desire to do things on our own is really a plea for help. We are crying for help because God intends for all of us to need each other. The most comforting thing to know, in any family, is that someone is on your side. God has guaranteed to be with us in times of sorrow, in times of sickness, and in times of human abandonment. But *how does God show Himself in times where we've been forsaken?* He appears through our neighbor. He shows up in the form of a helping hand. He comes to us through the affirmative words of a mother; in the giving hands of a father; in the comforting love of a daughter. God uses us, his people, as utensils of His love. The more we separate, the darker the world becomes. The more we divide ourselves into shattered pieces, the harder it becomes to see God clearly. However, when we unite, the world brightens. When we come together, God is glorified.

This chapter is all about refocusing your attention. I need to help you see what the church at Corinth couldn't see. Firstly, being "dependent" on your brother or needing your sister is not a sign of weakness; it's actually a sign of strength. It's an indication of strength because our confession of need reflects our dependence on Christ. When we ask for help, we are not just asking a person. We are asking God through the person. We are acknowledging that we can't live in this world by ourselves, so we need someone else to help us to make it.

Our love toward others is nothing but an echo and testimony that speaks back to our love for God. If you refuse to ask for help, you refuse to accept God's love. This is why the scripture commands us to love God and to love our neighbors as we love ourselves. Jesus does not separate the first commandment from the second. They both hold an equal weight of importance in God's mind.

> **IF YOU REFUSE TO ASK FOR HELP, YOU REFUSE TO ACCEPT GOD'S LOVE.**

We also must realize our role in helping others to get to God. You may work with someone who needs God, but they don't know how to ask for it. Or you may have a family member who is always sad, depressed, and low. What is your role as a mature Christian? You've got to bring the light to dark places and help others by bringing them closer to Jesus. It's not a good thing to worship God and leave your family in the dark. You'd be surprised to know how many parents will run to church and leave their children at home. It's amazing how we see people in need, and don't offer church but will quickly offer counseling.

Listen. When we run to the church to worship our God and we leave the family who desperately needs God, we make God a secret code that only we have access to. Don't hide God from the people who need him most. Your role in your family may be to help them come to know Christ. Don't become elitist and only hang out with people on "meat." Your wisdom will help to move someone from immaturity to maturity.

Remember, Jesus said in Matthew 9:12 "They that be whole need not a physician, but they that are sick." In other words, don't waste your time watering flowers that are already sprouting forth. Spend time cultivating the seed that can't grow because it's not yet exposed to the light. Pay attention to the sick, the broken, the destitute, and the disconnected. Our job as Christians is to mend the brokenhearted through the love of Jesus Christ, by extending love to all people; assuring them, most of all, that we are on their side.

> **DON'T WASTE YOUR TIME WATERING FLOWERS THAT ARE ALREADY SPROUTING FORTH.**

Does Your Heart Break for What Breaks God's Heart?

When you look at multiple cases of single mothers and single teens having multiple children, by multiple fathers; or when you look at the statistics of juveniles who are serving life sentences for crimes that they cannot undo, does your heart break? It should because our hearts should break for what breaks God's heart. Our hearts should break because nobody can fully comprehend why this epidemic has become so common in our cities.

We can't figure out why these violent occurrences keep happening. We can't figure out why gangs have become a norm in our society. Why are the young girls getting pregnant before they become college graduates? Why are young men wasting their lives selling drugs? Could it be that somewhere, someone forgot to look at them and say, "Listen, God has a greater plan for your life. You don't have to make these choices. You may feel alone but I am on your side." Maybe we forgot to look at the young women in our churches. How many times have we walked up to them and said, "God loves you. You don't have to use your body to communicate love. No matter what you've done, I am on your side. You don't have to live life as someone you were never meant to be; I am on your side."

> **OUR HEARTS SHOULD BREAK FOR WHAT BREAKS GOD'S HEART.**

No matter who we are and where we are in our lives, we all need somebody. We all hate to be the topic of discussion and never the object of affection. We all want to be loved. We all want to know that we matter. We all need to hear those words: *"I am on your side"* but more importantly, we need to BE those words.

Step In the Fire With Them

If we stepped up to the plate and realized our true call as "fire-proof" disciples, then we would produce more people after God's own heart. Look throughout the Bible. Seldom do we see prophets, pastors, evangelists, teachers, and women and men of faith producing great things in isolation. What we see is a people of likeminded faith, coming together and operating in oneness. Take the story of Shadrach, Meshach, and Abednego for instance. They didn't go into the fire alone. They stepped into the fire together. What does that teach us? Firstly, it shows us that power manifests when you enter the fire with your brother and sister. If you go alone, you just might burn up. But if you go together, great things can be accomplished. When two or three are gathered in His name, He will be in the midst. In other words, when we come together, the fire isn't as hot; the tribulation isn't as overwhelming; the circumstances aren't as unbearable. Why? Because we have someone we can go through the fire with; we have someone that we can rely on; we have someone we can cry on; we have someone we can vent to; someone who will understand our situation without judging us! When we go through things together, we have someone who can lay hands and pray for us when we can't pray for ourselves.

> **WE ALL HATE TO BE THE TOPIC OF DISCUSSION AND NEVER THE OBJECT OF AFFECTION.**

Think about another brother in the Bible by the name of Job. Job had friends. When Job was being tested, some of his friends gave negative advice, and others gave premature advice but guess what! Job wasn't by himself. At least he had someone to talk to! At least he had someone who was willing to stand next to him during times of great loss and death.

The story of Job teaches us a great lesson about being there for people during times of grief and pain. Sometimes, we just need to be silent and say nothing. Sometimes our words don't help. What if they just need you to "be there" for them? What if you don't need to find the right sermonette to preach? What if God is asking you to be His hands and feet and just show up for someone else, while they are being tried in the midst of their greatest fire?

> **THE TRUTH BEHIND ANY FRIENDSHIP WILL COME TO THE SURFACE DURING THE DIFFICULT TIMES.**

That's the entire point of this chapter. Don't be afraid to ask for help, and don't be afraid to tell someone, *"I am on your side."* The truth behind any friendship will come to the surface during the difficult times. As a friend, the way you respond and the way you react during my time of need will speak volumes to me about your loyalty. Are you willing to step into the fire with your brothers and sisters? Are you the individual to whom others can run to, when everyone else has walked out? Gone are the days when fulltime Christians are just part time friends. God wants you to be sold out to your friends the same way you are sold out to Christ.

When you have grown up in the faith, you should have the scent of someone else's fire. Your prayers should not just be about you; you should be interceding more than you are asking for anything. True evidence of a mature Christian is when they come before God holding someone else's broken pieces, and begging God to help them to put their friend's heart back together again.

> **YOU SHOULD HAVE THE SCENT OF SOMEONE ELSE'S FIRE.**

In Order to Have a Friend, Be a Friend

There is a line in the song, "I Need You to Survive" that says: *"it is His will that every need be supplied."* That line can be translated to mean this: the same way God expects you to be there for others, He also expects others to be there for you. Take a moment to think about a few close friends in your life. Name five people that have been there to support you through thick and thin. If you cannot come up with any names, then, my next question to you is: how friendly are you to others? When's the last time you've stepped into the fire for someone? How often do you extend your time and support? How discerning are you when they need you? Do you wait for them to call you or do you call them because the Holy Spirit has prompted you to do so?

In order to have a friend, you must first be a friend. It's foolish to think that you will gain a support system when you aren't supportive to anyone. God will not send someone to your rescue if you are always absent during someone else's struggle. So, if you've come to realize that you are alone every time the flames of tribulation spark in your life, then maybe it's because you refuse to help others during their time of need.

When you have endured the fire and you have grown beyond the pettiness of childish behavior, you should have a laundry list of references that can say for sure, *"this person is dependable."* You should have verifiable proof of your loyalty to others. Think about it. Paul was a great man of God but Silas helped him to pray. Mary was a great woman of God who carried JESUS for nine long months, but Elizabeth identified with her experience. Often times, all we need in life is an Elizabeth who looks like what we've been through. All we need is someone who can stand as a mirror reflection of where we are going and utter the words, "you can make it." We don't need homiletics, hermeneutics, or calisthenics; we just need a FRIEND! The better we are at becoming friends, the more believable we are when we say, "I'm a Christian." Don't just tell someone that you are sorry that they lost their mother. Don't just say the common line, "if there is something I can do, call me." You should know already that nobody in pain is going to call! Instead of making wounded hearts do the work, why not just show up and be there? Why not discern a need and bring food over to the house? No matter how sad we are, at some point, we all will have to eat! So pray and ask God to reveal how you can be present, instead of making other people feel your absence.

Pay a bill or two if you sense that your friend is suffering. Don't make the girl who just lost her job always have to ask for help. Chances are, they are too hurt to articulate their true needs. In fact, sometimes, they don't even know what they have need of, because their pain is blocking their coherence. No matter what others are going through, remember this: the best way to invite the presence of God to people, is to be the presence of God for people. In other words, be the hands and feet that Jesus uses to guide others to deliverance and restoration. Meet the need, sow the seed, and be the friend you've always prayed for. The moment you do, you'll see it coming right back to you.

> **THE BEST WAY TO INVITE THE PRESENCE OF GOD TO PEOPLE, IS TO BE THE PRESENCE OF GOD FOR PEOPLE.**

CHAPTER 8

NOTHING GROWS WITHOUT A PROCESS

1 Corinthians 3:4-6

For while one saith, I am of Paul; and another, I am of Apollos; are ye not carnal? Who then is Paul, and who is Apollos, but ministers by whom ye believed, even as the Lord gave to every man? I have planted, Apollos watered; but God gave the increase.

As a pastor, you must always be prepared at all times to help your parishioners. The pastoral call is a challenging call. You never know what's going to come across your desk. You never know from day to day, what phone calls you will receive. That's why it's so important to be sure of your calling, and not just excited about a position that seems glamorous. Remember, the call is not about the glitz of ministry, it's about the gospel of Jesus Christ. Those who are fit for the fire are also chosen to help others understand the purpose behind the process.

This chapter was inspired by a conversation I had with one of my deacons some time ago. He walked into my office complaining. He looked like he was about to take someone's head off. Of course, I figured he was about to vent for hours. It actually turned out to be a quick conversation.

"Pastor!" he began.

"Yes Deac—" I said as I motioned for him to sit down.

"I just don't know why you continue to keep some of these people on the church roll" he complained.

"What do you mean?" I inquired.

"I mean, these lackadaisical members. These inconsistent members. They come to church on Sunday and maybe on Wednesday, but when we have anything else at the church, you can never find them!" he yelled.

"Hmmm. Well, Deacon, I think you are looking at it from a one-sided perspective."

"What do you mean?" he asked.

"I mean this. As a pastor, I know that the church needs people like you—those who come to church regularly."

"Uh huh"

"But the church also needs those who work and are as quick to give as you are quick to praise."

"I see…"

"Scripture says… one plants, one waters, but God gives the increase. In regard to our church growing, both of you are just as important. Your role is to keep the spirit moving in the church. Another person's role may be to help keep the lights on in the church! Some people are quick to praise and less quick to give; and vice versa. So the church needs all members to do their part, and work together."

Needless to say, the issue was quickly resolved because I have a great deal of experience with this issue. I have preached to many people who have zeal but are stingy. And I also have pastored people who travel frequently, but they are faithful tithers. In order to move forward and in order to grow, every one must learn to be who they are, and serve God the way He has called us to serve. A good leader will see the big picture. That means he or she sees the problem and the solution from every perspective. In order to grow the house of God, pastors need *presence* and *presents*. We need ministry and money. Both components are working together to build the house of God. I urge you to stop trying to have everyone look like you and sound like you. If the church is so full of zeal and empty of financial support, then you will be having church in the park in a few months. But if the church is only money-focused and not spirit-led, then you don't have a church; you have a corporation. You have an elitist organization that is more concerned with monetary gain and not godly transformation.

> **IN ORDER TO GROW THE HOUSE OF GOD, PASTORS NEED PRESENCE AND PRESENTS.**

When Paul shifts the subject of his message in 1 Corinthians 3, he begins to talk agriculture. He speaks about two important factors that are necessary for any vision, team, or individual to grow. Paul speaks about *process* and *glory*. This chapter will focus on the *process*. You must understand that nothing in life will grow, mature, or change without a process. The process is the period of time that is allotted for any given thing to mature.

> **IF THERE IS NO SEED TO PLANT INTO THE GROUND, THEN YOU JUST HAVE A PUDDLE OF POTENTIAL.**

In the school system, the process of learning involves enrollment, assessment, evaluation, and graduation. You cannot obtain a degree without passing each part of the process. The same is true for human beings. We begin as infants, we learn to crawl, walk, talk, and then take over the world! The process of life is one of development, maturity, and transformation. If you want anything to grow, you've got to give it time to go through its own process.

Puddles of Potential

Paul recognized this when he says, "as a farmer I planted and Apollos, he watered but we were both needed for the process of growth." If Paul did not plant, Apollos could not have watered. And if Apollos did not water, nothing that Paul planted would've grown. So get this. No matter how much water exists in the church, if there is no seed to plant into the ground, then you just have a puddle of potential. And that is the problem with so many churches, families, businesses, and marriages today. We are puddles full of potential. We start out great but we don't complete. We have a vision but we don't have the help to grow the vision. Our greatest efforts are spent on things that aren't essential for growth. We buy a home before we make peace with our family members. We spend more time decorating the church than we do growing it. If you are fit to endure the fire, you are open to the process. Nothing happens overnight. Visions require time. Growth requires a process. If you are a puddle of potential, that means you have the excitement but not the knowledge. You have the degree but not the experience. You have the plans but not the finances. Without the seed, nothing will grow. If you do not pray for God to send laborers who will serve your vision, your vision will never get off the ground.

You can plant a vision for your family to sit for dinner all you want, but if your family doesn't show up for dinner, then your planting was in vain. You can plant a desire for your husband to take more initiative around the house, but if you aren't willing to also listen to his needs and adjust your attitude, then don't expect your relationship to grow. The fire teaches us to appreciate the process. The fire teaches us to endure the labor pains and growing seasons. You can only reap that which you have first sown. And you can't sow anything without seeds, water, and sunlight. It's the natural process of growth.

Sow Together, Grow Together

The reason we spent the last two chapters talking about praying for your enemies, and coming together is because, no matter how great you are as an individual, God requires us to work together. God requires us to join forces in order to make His will come to pass. The problem with many of us is that we are attracted to the one-man stage play. We want to be the public figure in the spotlight—the talk show host, the megachurch pastor, the charismatic entertainer-but we don't see the team behind the scenes. Every public figure has a team of invisible helpers watering their seeds of success. Think about your life. If it wasn't for the teacher who helped you to read, you wouldn't have become a lawyer. If it wasn't for your algebra teacher who helped you to do math, you wouldn't have become an accountant. If it wasn't for grandma's prayers, you might not be reading this book right now. But there was a team of water carriers helping you to grow in the process. There have always been helpers that have pushed you to become the greatest man or woman of God that you can be. Now, you've got to be able to see yourself as a part of a bigger vision than you. What if you never become the spotlight person? Does that make your role any less important? If you are prepared for the greater blessings, then you also need to know what your role is and what God is calling you to grow.

THE PROCESS TEACHES PATIENCE

James 1:2-4
My brethren count it all joy when ye fall into divers temptations; knowing this, that the trying of your faith worketh patience. But let patience have her perfect work, that ye may be perfect and entire, wanting nothing.

What do we gain from the process? What do processes teach us? Primarily, the process will teach you patience. Patience is the thing that most of us lack, and everybody can use a little more of it. Our lack of patience has been the primary reason that many of us are in debt. Our lack of patience has been the primary reason why so many of us jumped into a relationship that we didn't fully examine. Patience is a key virtue that can only be taught through a process. If you can't wait for it to grow, then you may forfeit your harvest. An impatient farmer will never make a lot of money. Patience produces ripe harvests. If the farmer pulls the plant out of the ground before its proper time, the fruit will not be able to serve its full purpose.

> **PATIENCE PRODUCES RIPE HARVESTS.**

After God teaches us love, longsuffering, endurance, unity, prayer and power, he must teach us patience. Why? So that we can become the mature Christians that He intends for us to be. They used to say, "anything worth having is worth waiting for." Well, the test of patience will surely teach you how to wait. It will also reveal to you people's true colors. If the man can't wait until marriage, then it's an indication of what his motives are. If a female can't wait until you propose, but instead, starts buying her own wedding dress before you meet her family, then you need to run toward the nearest exit as soon as possible. Patience teaches you how to distinguish a Christian on milk and a Christian on meat.

If you think about it, anybody can have faith enough to believe that God will do it. Anybody can believe that God can bring something to pass when it manifests immediately. The challenge, however, is when God asks you to believe for something to manifest and then forces you to wait for years and years and years. The challenge is for you to keep believing even though you, like Sarah, have passed the age where women can still have babies. If I could get every prayer answered overnight, I would pray all of the time. I would believe God for everything. But when God takes months and months at a time to respond to my prayer; or when my loved one doesn't heal as quickly as I want them to heal; or when I have to wait for the settlement money to come after years of pain, it can become a real challenge to trust God. This is why patience has to have her perfect work in it. No matter how big you think you are in the kingdom, the patience test comes to each and every one of us. God sends this test to strengthen our endurance, and to grow our faith. If we do not pass it, He will keep sending it our way until we do.

Chapter 9

Only God Gets the Glory!

1 Corinthians 3:7-8

So then neither is he that planteth any thing, neither he that watereth; but God that giveth the increase. Now he that planteth and he that watereth are one: and every man shall receive his own reward according to his own labour.

In the previous chapter, I said that Paul used the analogy of planting and watering for two reasons. First, he wanted the church to understand the growth process. Anything worth growing is also worth the process it takes for that thing to mature and develop. But secondly, Paul wanted to discuss the subject of glory. What do preachers mean when we speak of glory? What are praise and worship leaders asking for when they invoke the glory of the Lord? Most importantly, how does my understanding of glory help me while I'm standing in the midst of the fire?

To start off, let me say this: "glory" is a popular word used in many churches, so the meaning could vary depending on the speaker. But when Paul writes, "one plants, one waters, but God gives the increase," he's really saying, "Listen church, I know many of you helped to make this vision come to life, and I know you obtained a degree in this field, but at the end of the day... ONLY GOD GETS THE GLORY!" Only God gets the attention. Only God is worthy of an ovation. So if Oprah Winfrey calls the greatest award program in all of the world, and recommends your idea, your vision, your organization, or your family business, don't be surprised if they don't call your name at the ceremony. When the votes have been cast and the announcer says the winner's name, he or she will only call God's name and only God will have the honor of receiving the trophy. Why? Because only God gets the glory! Only God will receive the honor. And only God is due all the praise.

> **EVERYTHING WE GO THROUGH, MUCH LIKE THE EMAILS WE SEND, HAVE A SUBJECT LINE AND A SIGNATURE.**

DON'T GET IT TWISTED! IT'S NOT ABOUT YOU!

Every trial you face will either bring attention to you or to the God who made you. Everything we go through, much like the emails we send, have a subject line and a signature. At the end of all of your doing, sowing, reaping, helping, assisting, giving, sacrificing, and lending, God is the signature line that receives all of the glory. God is the endorser that makes your program possible. God is the sponsor behind your vision, helping it to receive the proper funding it needs to continue. Paul understands this, but the church does not. The people at Corinth are caught up in their contributions. They are caught up in their economic success. But Paul writes these words to say, in no uncertain terms,

"Don't get it twisted! God can use you; but ultimately, it's not about you."

When we speak about the glory of the Lord in this sense, we learn about another virtue that every believer must have in their fireproof backpack. That virtue is called humility. Glory is the main character of any movie; it's the big point to all that is said or done. To give glory to someone is to give credit to its creator. It's almost like saying, "Listen, I couldn't have done this without you." So how does this relate to humility? *I'm so glad you asked.*

In the kingdom, all of the glory *should* belong to God, right? Right! But if we are honest, that is not always the case. Just because people minister in God's name does not always mean that all glory actually goes to God! In fact, one of the primary disconnects in the church has to do with separating our ego from our assignment. In other words, we have to differentiate our desire to do what we want from the commitments that God has called us to. Everyday, we must crucify our flesh again and again. Everyday we must rid ourselves of the temptation to self-glory. Everyday we must remind ourselves that "my body is the temple of God," and most importantly, "I am not my own" (1 Corinthians 6:19). God uses us as vessels of honor, and not as tooters of our own horn. We do not belong to ourselves. Our wants don't control us. Our careers don't define us. We are instruments in God's orchestra. We are blades of grass in God's field. Every morning, we need to stand in the mirror of faith and remind ourselves of what we see. God has called us to be reflections of His glory. We should never take credit for ourselves, but instead, we should give all honor back to our Creator.

Remind yourself that you belong to God. That also means your children belong to God. Your spouse belongs to God. Your gifts and talents belong to God. You are not the proprietor of God's goods. You do not even own the house and the car that was placed in your name. If anything, all we own is a "thank you!" All we own is a "hallelujah," because if we look back over our lives, we will remember that God didn't have to bless us the way He has blessed us. We will remember the places we used to go, and the people we used to deal with, and we will pause and praise God for the things He has already delivered us from.

> **YOU ARE NOT THE PROPRIETOR OF GOD'S GOODS.**

Enroll in the Humility Academy

When you take a course in humility, God will sometimes allow you to be overlooked just to test out your motives. *I'm sure you know what I mean.* Sometimes He will allow the person who organized the program to thank everybody else except you; just to see how you will react. I'm telling you, you would be surprised to know how many people leave churches around the country all because the pastor didn't thank them for bringing peach cobbler to the church anniversary. You'd be surprised how many people thrive off of human validation, so much so that if they don't receive it, they feel as if you have abandoned them. Can't you see why Paul is talking so much about milk and meat? There are too many grown adults sucking on bottles! The immature Christian will walk out and leave. They easily forget that God was just putting them through a test.

Most times, this test of humility comes to us because God needs to check our motivation. He needs to make sure we are truly workers in His vineyard and not users in the church. We all know a few users. They show up at the family dinner asking for a few dollars. They show up at work when they need you to cover their shift at least three times a week. They show up in church, full of condescension and entitlement, expecting God to worship them. *Users*. They will work for you long enough to get unemployment, and then they will drop you like a penny in a wishing well. They will smile in your face and talk about you as if you didn't help them to become who they are. Users pretend to love God, but as soon as church is over, they run around to give out business cards and flyers to advertise their new business. Do you know a few users? If so, I recommend that you tell them to read this chapter on glory.

Until the body of Christ recognizes that we are only seeds in God's masterful garden, called to grow in the grace and knowledge of His love, we will always remain on the level we are on. Aren't you tired of the same old thing? Don't you want to be in another place with God? Well if you do, the first pill you have to swallow is that God will not share His glory! Only God will get the credit! And only God deserves the ovation.

> **EVERYBODY WANTS TO BE USEFUL; BUT NOBODY WANTS TO BE USED.**

Don't Overlook Anyone On Purpose!

In the previous section, I talked about users. I also said that God will sometimes test us by allowing us to be overlooked. But let me clarify something. Everybody wants to be recognized for the gifts they bring to any vision. Everybody wants to be useful; but nobody wants to be used. So don't overlook anyone on purpose! I don't want you to walk away from this chapter thinking that it is OK to intentionally overlook someone. After mommy sweats over that hot stove to cook dinner every night, the children need to say "thank you." After daddy labors on the job working two part time-jobs and a full-time job, mommy needs to pause from her favorite television show to say "thank you." Just because the scripture says that "God gives the increase," that does not give us a license to abuse people. We are all gifts to the body of Christ. God is looking for a people who will be humble enough to be overlooked, but thoughtful enough to say "thank you." I always find it interesting that the one who wants the most thanks is also the one who never says it. And the one begging for an appreciation service never shows up to anyone else's appreciation service. It's a paradox in the church. If you want to receive a blessing, you must be a blessing. If you want to have a friend, then you must be a friend. You must not only BE the change you want to see in the world, but you must be who you are called to be whether the world changes or not. God is looking for humble men and women of God who can walk through the fire and not have to tell everybody what they've been through.

> **HUMBLE ENOUGH TO BE OVERLOOKED, BUT THOUGHTFUL ENOUGH TO SAY "THANK YOU."**

Don't you just hate walking up to some people in church? All you want to say is "hello," and move on, but before you know it, they are venting about the laundry list of issues they've been through. This week, the dog died. The cat ate the fish. The fish burned in the grease. The grease wasn't good enough for the fried chicken; so she didn't eat for three days. She missed church for three days because the lights were turned off. And to top it all off, the garbage man ran over her bicycle!

Every once in a while, we've got to take some things to God in prayer. God did not call us to be dump trucks. He called us to be planters and helpers. Some water, some plant, and God gives the increase. The more we look for men and women to validate our garden, the more power we relinquish to them. The more control we allow others to have over our increase, the less glory God will receive from your harvest. Always remember: if you give a human being power over your increase, prepare for a decrease. Prepare for them to pull the plug on you when you least expect it; leaving you desperate, alone, and chasing after the garbage man for your bicycle!

> **THE MORE WE LOOK FOR MEN AND WOMEN TO VALIDATE OUR GARDEN, THE MORE POWER WE RELINQUISH TO THEM.**

God Will Not Share His Glory

God knows what He is doing. He knows that humans can't handle too much praise, because if we do receive it, we will get caught up in ourselves. Like Lucifer, we will assume that we have just as much power as God. The truth is, however, that we don't! Readers, beware of the self-righteous spirit that creeps into the heart, making us think that we are better than someone else. Anytime a human being takes God's glory, we end up creating idols that point to us, and not Christ. Consider Isaiah 42: 8: *I am the LORD: that is my name: and my glory will I not give to another, neither my praise to graven images.* Is it clear? Do you get it? God will not, under any circumstances, share His glory with another.

This is why Paul talks about the process of growth in 1 Corinthians. If Apollos had possessed all of the gifts to do everything himself, then Apollos would have wanted some glory. If Paul had been able to write the letters, lay hands on the sick, feed the poor, settle disputes with kings, and cook breakfast, lunch and dinner, then Paul would've, no doubt, become puffed up in his own works. Paul would've forgotten the God who empowered him in the first place.

> **BE CAREFUL NOT TO BECOME TRICKED BY YOUR OWN TALENTS.**

This is why I pray long and hard for people in ministry who have multiple talents. If God has given you many gifts, be careful not to become tricked by your own talents. If you buy into your own press, and if you start believing your own hype, you will build an empire of "self-glory" thinking that you run the world. But that is the farthest thing from the truth. The truth is, God has invested in you so that you can invest into others. The truth is, no matter how many gifts you have—whether you can sing, write, preach, dance, and play the trumpet while beating the drums—there is always something in the garden that you cannot do. There is always a weakness lurking nearby your bushes of strength. Do not get so caught up in yourself that you forget the Giver of every gift, and the Maker of all true ministry.

A Thorn With Your Name on It

Maybe you are reading this and wondering why God has not lifted your burden. Maybe you have a leadership weakness that forces you to depend on someone else. Maybe you are frustrated because you are growing in so many areas, but there is one issue that won't seem to go away. If that is the case, then my question to you is, what if God planted that weakness or allowed that idiosyncrasy to exist so that you wouldn't steal his glory? What if God did not remove the thorn from Paul because God knew that Paul would get caught up in himself? Don't take my word for it. Read it for yourself! This is what Paul says after asking God to take the thorn away three times!

2 Corinthians 12:7-10

And lest I should be exalted above measure through the abundance of the revelations, there was given to me a thorn in the flesh, the messenger of Satan to buffet me, lest I should be exalted above measure. For this thing I besought the Lord thrice, that it might depart from me. And he said unto me, My grace is sufficient for thee: for my strength is made perfect in weakness. Most gladly therefore will I rather glory in my infirmities, that the power of Christ may rest upon me. Therefore I take pleasure in infirmities, in reproaches, in necessities, in persecutions, in distresses for Christ's sake: for when I am weak, then am I strong.

A few chapters ago, we talked about the necessity of suffering. Here again we see how suffering works in our favor. Suffering keeps us humble. Suffering keeps us human. Paul is blessed with many gifts. He can see visions and he has the gift of knowledge. He can also write to various churches and settle disputes, but despite all of these great qualities, God allows Paul to endure the pain of a thorn. Why? So that Paul does not glory in himself. He does all of this so that Paul does not exalt himself above measure.

> **WHEN GOD WANTS TO SECURE HIS GLORY, HE WILL BLESS YOU WITH A STRUGGLE.**

Here's the point: when God wants to secure His glory, He will bless you with a struggle. He will give you a thorn, and then smother you in grace. He will make the vision so big that you will need to ask for help. He will tell you to speak publicly and then give you a speech impediment so that you, like Moses, can turn to others, like Aaron, to help you. When God wants to make sure that you understand the process, He will produce within you a desire to combine forces. All of this will have one purpose in mind: so that God can get the glory.

PUT YOUR FOOT DOWN!

Don't forget that Paul is not just talking to the church at Corinth as a spiritual leader. At this point, he is speaking to them as their spiritual father. Paul is telling them, "you cannot obtain an abundant life in God if you are immature." Then he moves into planting and growing. These are lessons from the heart of a father. Paul has grown in the faith and will not allow them to remain stagnant. What we learn from Paul in this chapter is that God's glory comes to empower us. We are empowered, then, to instruct others. In essence, it happens like this. When God glorifies himself in you, He will always call you to bring people up higher. Do not allow your friends to settle. When you realize that God is using you to bring glory to His name, you've got to move from the comfort zone and enter into the correction zone. Entering into the correction zone means that we will speak to people in a loving manner, but sometimes we will have to use a fatherly/motherly tone. Sometimes we will have to correct them in kindness, but rebuke them in love. After we have grown up, and after God receives the glory from our lives, He will then plant within us a desire to spread the good news.

When God promotes you and gives you permission to correct others, make sure your love is genuine. Make sure they feel your sincerity. Let them know that you are on their side, but never compromise the word of God. As a mature man or woman, you have to correct what God reveals. And because you are on their side, you must not call right, wrong and you must not call wrong, right. My compassionate heart will not accept your chaos. My loving smile will not overlook your sin. Paul does not bite his tongue. He learned how to help others to endure the fire by turning up the heat in his conversation. Sometimes you will have to do the same. I know it will be a heated debate when you talk to your teenage daughter about what God expects from her dating choices, but you are planting a seed inside of her so that God can yield increase. Do not fear their faces. Do not bite your tongue. Instead, be who God has called you to be. Remind them that, "I'm saying this because I love you, I only want God to get the glory out of your life." The more we humble ourselves and help others to see God, the more we will see God's glory springing forth in our own lives. Never forget: all of the glory belongs to Him, and to whom much is given, much is also required.

Chapter 10

Building on a Solid Foundation

1 Corinthians 3:9-11

For we are labourers together with God: ye are God's husbandry, ye are God's building. According to the grace of God which is given unto me, as a wise masterbuilder, I have laid the foundation, and another buildeth thereon. But let every man take heed how he buildeth hereupon. For other foundation can no man lay than that is laid, which is Jesus Christ.

Stephanie and Tom were college sweethearts. He was the quarterback at one of the top Division 1 schools in the country. She was the captain of the cheerleading team. On the day they met, they took one look at each other and knew they would be head over heels for each other. It was "love at first sight." In two months, they were planning a wedding. In two years, they were expecting their first child. Two months after their first child was born, they moved into a brand new house.

They are now ten years into the marriage, and they are miserable. Three kids later, a summer home and two luxurious cars parked in the garage, everyone would think they are the happiest family around. But the truth is, they do not even sleep in the same bed together. Their children can tell that they are not friends. Their family doesn't bother to invite them to holiday dinners because one of them will end up arguing. Life for Tom is sad, grueling, and depressing. He spends most of his days working overtime just to stay out of the house for a little while longer. Stephanie pours her attention into the children, hoping that the children will help her to stay in a marriage that is currently on life support.

This story is no different than stories you may know. It's interesting how quickly someone can fall in "love," and yet, how quickly love can turn into hate. We call it "love at first sight," but maybe it's "lust at first sight". And now, the man who once sat by the fireplace with you and talked endlessly, is sitting across the dinner table in silence. He spends more time texting and emailing than he does talking and laughing. And the woman who used to cook and clean for her man is now ordering meals "To Go" and shopping herself into an addiction; all because she built her marriage on a faulty foundation.

How is your building doing?

If you look at any marriage statistic, you will discover startling news. Not only have 50 percent of all marriages ended in divorce, but many of those marriages included Christians as well. Why is this the case? *Who really knows.* There could be many factors that lead to marital dysfunction. But I believe the primary issue with all relationships—be they romantic, platonic, business, or otherwise—is that people fall in love with an "idea" of matrimony, but they don't spend time building a strong foundation. Most people are attracted to the "outside layers" of a relationship, but they do not set internal expectations. They tell each other what they *want* in a man or what they *want* in a woman, but they don't spend time expressing their needs. There is absolutely no way that any relationship can thrive without both parties knowing each other's expectations. The marriage that lasts is not lasting because he feels butterflies everyday. It doesn't endure the rough times because she is always excited to see her man after work. If this is the case for you, then you are the exception to the rule. But more often than not, the marriage that lasts is the one that lays a proper foundation. Each person will hold each other accountable by making sure that God is first in all things.

Is Jesus at the Center?

Many couples claim to love each other, but God is not at the center of their relationship. It's a sad thing to see any covenant go bad, but before we ask the gossip questions like—*Is he cheating? Are they happy? Who did what? Does she have a prenuptial agreement?*—the more important questions are: *Was their foundation cemented in Christ? Did they start the relationship on the right foot? How often did they pray together? How much did they seek God about whether this was the partner that He ordained?*

Readers, be careful not to build your life on a shifty foundation. Here I am using marriage as an example, but this is applicable to any relationship. If Jesus is not at the center of your company, your family, or your vision, it will fail. It may start off well, but you will see a drastic shift in the coming years. No matter how strong you think you are, and no matter how beautiful the exterior of the house may be, if your foundation is shaky, then your walls will fall apart little by little.

> **BE CAREFUL NOT TO BUILD YOUR LIFE ON A SHIFTY FOUNDATION.**

In 1 Corinthians 3, Paul isn't done with giving fatherly advice. He moves from planting and watering to another analogy that many of his listeners would've understood. He talks about the building process. He comes at it from an architectural standpoint. I'm sure you know what it takes to build a structure. First, you need an architect to come in and sketch out a blueprint. Then, you need the right materials to build the structure. But before any windows are purchased, and before we pick out the carpet or design the staircase, we've got to concentrate on the foundation. Foundation is everything!

When you build a foundation, you are not just throwing a little cement on the ground and leveling out the uneven places. Sometimes the ground is so bad that you have to dig up before you can fill in. Sometimes the area that you want to build on is toxic and contaminated. So, you have to inspect the grounds and fumigate the land before you even think about building your 40-story executive suite. Things have to be dug up before they can be built upon.

The way we understand digging up in the natural, also applies to the spiritual. When we ask ourselves, "where did I go wrong in this relationship?," perhaps the answer is you were trying to build on unleveled ground. Maybe you were trying to fill something in that hadn't yet been dug out. Maybe God was trying to teach you patience, but you were so adamant about making it happen that you ignored all of the warning signs.

YOU HAVE TO DIG UP BEFORE YOU CAN FILL IN.

Temporary Placeholders

Maybe you built your entire life on quicksand. It's a hard truth to accept, but if you look around today and nothing you sowed into is around to love you back, then your investments were built on quicksand. If you have no friends that you can count on, maybe your foundation was shaky from the beginning. It's a terrible thing to waste all of your emotional and financial investments on something that was not built to last. It's a horrible feeling to give permanent devotion to temporary placeholders. *You know what placeholders are.* They are the people in our lives that only get our attention because we have nothing else better to do. They are conversations we hold when we just need someone to talk to for a moment, but we have no intention of going deeper than where we are. Placeholders are people we date until our real spouse shows up. They are jobs we occupy just to have some spare change, but everyday we go to work knowing that we do not want to be there.

Paul wants to deliver his people from the placeholder mentality. He wants to move them beyond one good sermon, and help them to see their role in the building process. The first thing they need to do is see Jesus as the only foundation. They cannot build a community based on background, experience, resume, hard work, or stunning looks. They have to build their community on Christ. Consider the text: *According to the grace of God which is given unto me, as a wise masterbuilder, I have laid the foundation, and another buildeth thereon. But let every man take heed how he buildeth hereupon. For other foundation can no man lay than that is laid, which is Jesus Christ.* Paul is trying to get them to understand who Jesus is. Jesus is the author and finisher of our faith. Jesus is the chief cornerstone. Without Jesus as your

> IT'S A TERRIBLE THING TO WASTE ALL OF YOUR EMOTIONAL AND FINANCIAL INVESTMENTS ON SOMETHING THAT WAS NOT BUILT TO LAST. IT'S A HORRIBLE FEELING TO GIVE PERMANENT DEVOTION TO TEMPORARY PLACEHOLDERS.

foundation, you have nothing. In Paul's mind, Jesus is the best foundation that ever existed. I agree unequivocally with Paul. If you're going to build a business, let Jesus be the foundation; not your money. If you're going to build a family, let Jesus be the foundation; not your feelings. Feelings will come and go. But Jesus is the same yesterday, today and forevermore.

If you're going to build a ministry, don't build it on people. People will love you today and hate you within the hour. Build your ministry on Jesus. There is no other foundation that men should build on, other than that of Christ. Anything that I build on from this day forward, will have Jesus as the foundation of it. Declare today, "I will build my work on Jesus. I will build my hope on Jesus. My faith is built on Jesus because He is the only one that will never walk out." Build your hope on things eternal! Hold to God's unchanging hand!

If Jesus is my foundation, I can go through near-death experiences and I can still stand. I can stand because I am building my salvation on a strong foundation. All that we have been through this year should have taken us out! It should have made us lose our mind! It should have made us quit in the process! But we are still standing by the grace of God! We did not build our salvation on good things happening, we built it on Jesus.

You are a Co-Laborer with God

The second thing Paul wants to do, after showing them who Jesus is, is show them who they are. He wants them to understand their role in the kingdom. I am convinced that much of our drama in church will cease when more and more people come into the knowledge of their assignment. Listen to what Paul says: "...as a wise master builder I have laid the foundation and another buildeth thereon." The first thing he wants them to know is that he is only one part of the picture. Paul does his job but it's up to them to build on what he laid. So, the pastor may preach a word on Sunday, but it's up to you to live it. Your mother can pay your tuition, but it's up to you to do the work so that you can graduate. The pastor is not called to police you into surrender. We aren't called to check every decision you make. Once the Word has been spoken to you, you must build on top of that foundation.

Your devotion to God cannot be contingent upon another man. In other words, if you base your salvation on the pastor or the preacher, then you will not last. If you only come to church because your mate comes to church, you will not last. If you only come around when God blesses you with a new house or a new car, you will not last. If you're the type of Christian that can only be on time if you have a position or a title, you will not last. You are a builder with Christ. You have to see yourself as more than a servant. You are a co-worker with God! 1 Corinthians 3:9 says it bluntly: *For we are labourers together with God: ye are God's husbandry, ye are God's building.*

Do you realize what this means? It means that God does not call you his subordinate slave; He calls you a co-worker. He calls you a fellow builder. It also means that we all need to be delivered. We have to get delivered from *depending* on people all of the time. Yes, we need people to survive, but people are not our source. They are not our foundation. God is the only one who gets the glory, and God expects us to do the work so that His glory can be realized in the earth! Gone are the days when we treat God like a welfare office. We have to put in the work in order to receive our reward. Gone are the days when grown men can mooch off of their mother for 30 years and never pay rent. Eventually, you're going to have to put in some work! Turn off the video games and get a real job. Turn off Facebook and get in God's book.

YOU CAN'T MAKE THE DREAM A REALITY IF YOU REFUSE TO WAKE UP.

The time has come for us to work with God. The time has come for us to build a lasting structure. Whether that structure is a church, a family, or a dream, you can't make the dream a reality if you refuse to wake up. If you are fit to endure the fire, then you are ready to do the work. You don't live everyday expecting Oprah to give you a car. You don't live every second looking for a giveaway that you didn't earn. You are ready to work. Your hands are set to the plow. Your mind is always thinking about how to make the next part of the plan come together.

Think on any successful millionaire that you may know or one you've read about. Their days never end. When you see them on television, you see a public persona. But behind closed doors, they are working with co-laborers to help them build the dream. They don't have time for lazy workers. They don't have time for procrastinators.

Don't you hear what God is saying to you? It's time to change your focus and guard your time. If you want to see it happen in your lifetime, then you've got to get to work! You've got to discipline yourself to accomplish a little piece of the project each day. You can plan all day. You can dream all night. But if you never sit down and write the first chapter, then you will never become the bestselling author that you desire to be. Your vision can only become as big as the hands God uses to build it. If you do not see yourself as a co-worker today, then don't expect your vision to work for you tomorrow.

Chapter 11

YOU ARE FIT!

1 Corinthians 3:12-13

Now if any man build upon this foundation gold, silver, precious stones, wood, hay, stubble; Every man's work shall be made manifest: for the day shall declare it, because it shall be revealed by fire; and the fire shall try every man's work of what sort it is.

When fashion models prepare to walk the runway, I'm sure they look into the mirror one last time and think, "Do I look fat in this? Should I have skipped breakfast this morning?" When Olympians get ready to compete, I'm sure they have second doubts about whether they can run, jump, or swim against some of the greatest athletes in the world. Think about Gabrielle Douglas, for instance. Not only was she very young, and not only was the 2012 Olympics her first international competition, but she was a middle-class African-American girl. Her mother was a single parent. Her funds were extremely low. The odds were against her, and very few people thought she would win. She probably didn't even think she could win. She had never seen an African-American Olympian win in the field of gymnastics. She never knew what winning gold even felt like. But in the end, she became the first!

What if God is calling you to be the first in your family?

What do you do when God tells you to do something that nobody else has done? How do you explain a dream to your family that nobody else understands? No matter how qualified Gabby was, she needed some reassurance. She needed a word from her coach. She already had the skillset to win the gold, but skills without assurance will cause you to live beneath your means.

> **SKILLS WITHOUT ASSURANCE WILL CAUSE YOU TO LIVE BENEATH YOUR MEANS.**

How does all of this apply to you? *I'm so glad you asked.* It applies because you may be reading this book as a Gabby Douglas in your own field. You are full of skills and yet, you are living beneath your means. You are qualified to be the owner of the company, but you are settling for the entry-level position. You are ready to be married, but you are afraid to step out on faith.

By now, whether you realize it or not, you have been equipped with all that you need to succeed. You have been empowered to endure the fire. You have learned key principles like love, patience, endurance, stability, unity, prayer, and contentment, but you will never step into the fire without the fire jacket of assurance. You will never apply for the job if you are not confident that you are worth hiring. You will never go on that first date if you are not confident that he or she will find you attractive. Consider this chapter a course on confidence.

HAVE CONFIDENCE IN GOD!

Chapter 11 is your confidence booster. Jesus Christ, your life coach, is looking down from heaven with one word of assurance: YOU ARE FIT! God has tracked your performance, He has worked on your muscular strength, He has been in the gym with you; training you every single day for this moment. This moment will change your life. This moment will change your paradigm. The idea that God has given you will change the world for the better. Today, God is giving you permission to go after it. Today, He is granting you access. He's saying to you, "receive the harvest that comes after you have endured the fire." You are fit to move forward. You are fit to inherit the prize.

> **DON'T QUIT BEFORE YOU SEE THE FRUIT OF YOUR FIRE.**

This is not the time to let insecurity win. Today is not the day to talk yourself out of God's best. Just wake up and look in the mirror and declare who you are. You are the head and not the tail. You are above and not beneath. You are the lender and not the borrower. You are the favored son or daughter of God. You are an heir and joint heir to the throne. You deserve God's best and you will not settle for average.

Say to yourself, "I am fit; and because I am fit, I will not quit." You are almost at the gate of reward; don't quit before you see the fruit of your fire. Don't quit before you see the outcome. When the coach tells you that you can go to the Olympics, get on the plane and go to the Olympics! If the coach tells you that you are prepared for the race, put on your running shoes and get ready to win. Trust the coach enough to go after what He promised you. Trust God enough to apply for the PhD, even though your test scores are low. Trust God enough to stand before the judge, even though your criminal record is haunting you. God is bigger than the secrets that haunt us. God is bigger than your credit score. God is with you, and God is for you. Even though you are walking through the valley of the shadow of death, don't forget that God is the light of the world! Don't forget that God's grace is bigger than your guilt. God can drop the charges. God can turn the marriage around. God can approve you for the home.

> **GOD'S GRACE IS BIGGER THAN YOUR GUILT.**

IT'S A NEW DAY!

Today is a new day. Today, God is changing the wind current of your life. Today, God is shifting you into a new moment. He's causing your enemies to bless you. He's allowing your past to catapult you into a prosperous future. Pure blessings and much fruit are heading your way. That's why you must be confident. You must have your assurance muscles in tact. Your confidence is your fuel. Your confidence is your confirmation. If a teacher stands up before his class and whispers timidly in front of them, they will assume that he cannot teach. Why? Because his voice and posture do not reflect his experience, potential and power.

The same is true for you. God wants his people to have confidence in Him. You need to get up, dust yourself off, and walk boldly in God's promises. Your posture of confidence will bring a new glory in your home. Your posture of confidence will cause people to respect you. Our confidence in God is the crazy glue that puts faith and works together. Faith without works is dead, so we can't produce for God until we believe that God has made us fit to do it. At the same time, no matter how much faith we have, if we do not put some work on the table, our faith cannot yield results. Your bold faith without confident works is dead.

This is also a new day of trust. It is not enough to simply trust in the Lord; we must also trust the God that resides inside of us. We need to trust that God's word is true. God will never leave us nor forsake us. God has been preparing us for greater works, and he is relying on us to bring a greater understanding of who He is to those who don't know Him. If you do not hear anything else that I write in this book, I need you to hear these words and receive them: YOU ARE FIT!

GET A REVELATION!

By verse 13, Paul has already identified Jesus as the foundation. Remember, Jesus is the centerpiece of all that we do. He is the one who brings all things together. He is the beginning, the middle and the end. With that in mind, Paul says, *"Now if any man build upon this foundation gold, silver, precious stones, wood, hay, stubble; every man's work shall be made manifest:"* In other words, Paul is saying, "you are what you build." You become what you focus on. The first set of items— the gold, silver, and precious stones—are items that must go through fire in order to become what they are. If you look at gold before it goes through its process, it actually looks like dirt. It looks filthy and dull. But as soon as you expose it to heat, it will burn and that burning process will cause it to shine.

Remember, you are what you build. So if you're going through a heated situation, get ready to shine! If friends have burned you, then get ready to shine! If you've been grinding for years, prepare for the glory. After you have suffered a little while, there shall be glory! After you have built a house on proper foundation, you can have confidence that it will not fall to the ground. They may have burned your flesh, but they cannot touch your spirit. You may have lost the house, but your gold shines brighter than a house or a car. Your gold is in the revelation of who God is!

Do you remember the story of Peter? Do you remember that Peter identifies Jesus as, "the son of the living God?" After that, Jesus says, "flesh and blood did not reveal this to you." Of course, flesh and blood did not reveal it to Peter! Peter got a revelation about God. He got a new understanding of who God was. That's what trials do for us. They give us a new understanding about God. At some point in the journey, Peter understood something new that the other disciples didn't. A new revelation led him to a new declaration. And a new declaration led him to promotion.

Jesus promotes Peter by saying, "your name is no longer Peter, but it's Petros; (which means rock) and upon this rock, I will build my church." That rock was the rock of revelation. Once you know Jesus, you can build. Once you know Jesus, God will change your name. Revelation is a game changer. What people call you will change. How people see you will change. So, prepare for the name change. Prepare for your surroundings to change. Prepare for the vision to change. Prepare for the abundant life you've been waiting for. God is testing your materials all because you've got a revelation. And now that you have that revelation, you are positioned for promotion.

Prepare for Next Level Living

Promotion is a great thing to shout about, but don't get it twisted! Promotion will not exempt you from the attacks of the enemy. Promotion does not cause the enemy to disappear from your life. That's why Jesus says, "upon this rock I will build my church and the very gates of hell shall not prevail against it." That word 'prevail' means to succeed or to conquer. So God is saying, "yes, you will go through the fire, but the fire will not go through you." In other words, you will experience attacks against your vision, but your vision will not falter. Your plans will not collapse. Everything that God has promised you, will still come to pass. Why? Because God is the coach that has said three words: YOU ARE FIT. God is the architect who is overseeing your building. God is the lawyer who has walked into the courtroom of life and said, "Drop the charges!"

> **"YES, YOU WILL GO THROUGH THE FIRE, BUT THE FIRE WILL NOT GO THROUGH YOU."**

Prepare yourself for next level living. You will go through storms, but you will not be overtaken. Every day will not be a sunny day, but the tsunamis and tornadoes will not come nigh thee. It's time to let your work, work for you. It's time to enjoy the fruits of your labor. It is time to mount the podium and claim your gold medal.

Save your Energy and Study your Enemy

Do you remember how we began this book? We talked about the boxing match that didn't end the way anyone expected it to. Floyd Mayweather was in the ring ducking, dodging, and taking hits. He was saving up energy, but he did get some bruises along the way. Nevertheless, he stayed in the fight and he endured the tribulation. He learned the art of war: to save your energy and study your enemy. You should be encouraged by this. If you are fit, you don't have to prove yourself to anyone. Save your energy. You don't have to tell everyone how much money you have in the bank. Save your energy. I know the haters are talking about you, but don't waste one text message giving ammunition to their drama. Save your energy, conserve your power, and study your opponent.

When you study your enemy, you learn his tactics. When you study your enemy, your confidence level goes up. If you go into the ring trying to show off your power, you will end up on the floor. You will end up in the hospital with a concussion. But if your foundation is in tact, then Jesus is fighting for you. If your foundation is in order, then God would never lead you to the ring unless He planned for you to win.

SAVE YOUR ENERGY, CONSERVE YOUR POWER, AND STUDY YOUR OPPONENT.

Claim the Victory!

At the end of the fight, Floyd threw one punch and claimed the victory. I know this year has been a hard year, but you are in the final rounds. This is the most important fight of your life. Don't let the enemy win. Claim the victory. Yes, you will have to duck, dodge, and take a few blows. Yes, you may have lost focus because you weren't aware of the power you had inside. But now that you know who God has called you to be, throw your punch. Knock the devil out of your marriage! Knock the devil out of your mind! Knock the devil out of your church! Knock the devil out at your job! Don't hit a supervisor or anything, but knock the devil out in the spirit!

Where the enemy is fighting you, knock the devil out. Where the enemy is tempting you, knock the devil out. One punch in the spirit, can change everything in the natural. Because you are fit for the fire, you can endure this fight. Save your energy. Study your enemy. Focus on the big picture, and get a revelation. If you do, your revelation will lead you to a declaration. And your declaration will lead you to promotion.

> **YOUR REVELATION WILL LEAD YOU TO A DECLARATION.**

When the enemy comes knocking on your door, tell him, "I can't talk now. I'm busy preparing for the greatest promotion of my life!"

Chapter 12

A Reward With My Name On It

1 Corinthians 3:14-15

If any man's work abide which he hath built thereupon, he shall receive a reward. If any man's work shall be burned, he shall suffer loss: but he himself shall be saved; yet so as by fire.

As a child, one of the best feelings in the world is finding out that you have mail. Remember what that felt like? Remember the joy of opening your first acceptance letter or getting a postcard from a family member in another country? As children, we loved mail because none of the mail we received were bills. As we grew older, we developed a strong dislike for getting the mail. Why? Because stacks of mail meant stacks of bills. Stacks of mail meant stacks of responsibility. And that is how it is in the kingdom. The more responsibility you have, the more you have to pay. The Bible says it like this, "to whom much is given, much is required." I know you may have been exposed to the greatness that ministry brings, but please do not forget that every envelope with your name on it, comes with a bill called responsibility attached to it.

The Good News and the Not-So-Good News

Just like Paul wrote to the church at Corinth, I am writing this final chapter because I do not want you to be ignorant. I do not want you to be deceived. In order to have a full understanding of the season you are in, you must know the good news and the not-so-good news. The good news is, God has a reward with your name on it. The not-so-good news is, that reward will cost you your life. In other words, you've got to be willing to give it your all in order to gain it all.

> **YOU'VE GOT TO BE WILLING TO GIVE IT YOUR ALL IN ORDER TO GAIN IT ALL.**

Let's talk about the good news first. I'll begin by saying that God is most pleased when we go through the fire, especially when we come out not looking like what we've been through. God rewards the patient and kind at heart. He loves it when His people do not complain about their struggles, but instead, we turn them into a sermon on hope. God loves a cheerful giver. So every time we give of our money, our time, or our energy, He blesses us with a reward. He writes a check in our name and puts it in the mailbox in front of our home. My check might read, "healing." Your check might read "deliverance." But whatever our reward is, He's given it to us because we've earned it. The scripture is clear. If the work you do endures the fire, and if you build a strong foundation in Christ, then the reward is guaranteed.

WELCOME TO YOUR REWARD

In the previous chapter, I talked about the process of gold and the reward that comes with it, but let me also share with you the benefits of silver and precious stones. Silver has been used as a form of currency by more people throughout history than any other metal, even gold. It was, in fact, one of the earliest metals known to mankind. But silver is also equated with suffering. It is a symbol of pain. Jesus, as you know, was sold for 30 pieces of silver. The process of making silver is a painful process. If you want to manufacture it, you have to crush silver ore into small pieces. The crushing process is necessary so that the material can become spongy or porous. Once crushed, the silver must be heated as well. Just like gold, the heat will re-form the material, making it become whatever the builder had in mind from the beginning.

If you are ever afforded the opportunity to suffer with Him, then you are also blessed with the reward of reigning with him. Don't always see suffering as a bad thing. It is the silver lining that helps you to take on a new form. Your marriage may be suffering right now, but let God re-form it. Your business may be suffering, but if it's built on Jesus, it can be resurrected. Your reformation is on the way. Your silver will be formed by the Manufacturer, and the Manufacturer will make you into the man or woman that He predestined you to be.

Paul then speaks about precious stones. Diamonds, for example, are precious stones. But did you know that diamonds in their first stage look like dark blocks of coal? Did you know that you can easily overlook a diamond because it is covered in blackness? But do not fear! Just because someone overlooked your value doesn't mean that you have no substance. They weren't anointed to see the true you! Everyone who walked out of your life, walked out because they saw your first stages. But God knew your finished product. God saw the diamond; they saw the coal. God saw the destiny on you; they saw the dirt on you. But after you have gone through the fire, you shall come forth! That is the reward of suffering. Every time you endure the flames of life, you qualify to receive the flood of God's favor. Welcome, my brothers and sisters, to the reward!

Everything Comes with a Cost

The not-so-good news is that everything comes with a cost. You definitely need to rejoice in your reward, but remember that God is requiring more from you. Now that you are mature, you have to change your attitude. Now that you have grown up, you have to maintain a consistent prayer life. Now that you are on meat and not milk, you have to live like a leader and not just sound like one. That is the cost of the reward. I said it before and

I'll say it again. Many people are in love with the glory that comes with ministry, but they don't want to go through the story that produces the glory.

The story of Lazarus is a perfect example. Mary, Martha and Lazarus were a family who wanted relationship with God without being tested. Mary and Martha loved their brother Lazarus. When Lazarus died, they became shocked and sad. Grief hit their household. Suffering knocked on their door. And when Jesus didn't bring the mail when they expected it, this added to their pain. They became upset and discouraged; all because Jesus did not come according to their plans.

> **JESUS WON'T BEND HIS WILL TO ACCOMMODATE OUR WANTS.**

As the recipient of God's reward, never forget your place. God is the giver of the gift; you are just the recipient. You don't get to call the shots, God does. You don't get to tell Jesus when to show up! Jesus will show up on His schedule, not yours. Jesus won't bend His will to accommodate our wants. God is God. And God will show up when your issue has produced maximum glory. I know you have been elevated in one area, but what if God needs you to suffer a little while longer in another area? What if God is looking at your situation and saying, "you need more fire to produce more glory."

The not-so-good side to the reward is that God might

throw you back in the fire tomorrow. Not only does He put us through multiple fires, but He loves to turn the flame up when He wants to make something special out of us. Think about the baker who wants to make the perfect pound cake. In order for the cake to rise to perfection, the baker cannot remove the pan a moment too soon. If the baker takes the cake out before its appointed time, the cake will crumble. The process will be stifled, and most importantly, it will not be ready for proper use.

> **THE LAST THING YOU WANT IS TO GET OUT OF YOUR PROCESS BEFORE TIME.**

Likewise, the last thing you want is to get out of your process before time. Everyone reading this book is reading it from a different moment of process. Don't jump out in the middle of "Ministry Street" without proper preparation. Allow God to keep you in His oven of testing until the time is right. The fire may be hot, but God's timing is perfect. God will never put us in the oven before our time, and He won't keep us in there longer than we need to be.

YOU MUST RISE!

I don't know what you are going through as you read this book, but I'm sure of one thing: this is your season of resurrection. This is your season to endure the flames of life in order to produce the best you that could ever be known. It's time to rise above the doubt, rise above the fear, rise above the haters, and rise above the tears. It's time to rise above insecurity and rise above depression. It's time to rise above generational curses and rise above self-condemnation.

In this season of rising, you will resurrect new strength and you will discover new wisdom. In this season of rising, the old nature will die and the new creature will live. In this season, your desires will change and the impure things that used to imprison you will burn away in the fire. God knows how to make us rise. If fire is the substance He uses to make you, then allow Him to let the fire reshape you into the instrument you are destined to be! It's time to rise above the ashes of your yesterday and leap straightway into your destiny.

No longer will you sit stagnated. No longer will you accept the lies that the enemy has whispered in your ear. No longer will you belittle yourself and deny the power of God that is working in you. As you read these words, God has strengthened you to endure the fire. He has equipped you with the virtue and tenacity necessary to keep moving forward. It's time to rise.

After you rise, there will be a full manifestation of God's power. After you rise, the reward will reveal itself. After you rise, God will update your charts and healing will come. Charges will be dropped. Marriages will be restored. Families will be reunited. Love will outlive hate. Strength will enter your weak places. Struggle will lose its appetite. Sin will loose its stronghold. You will rise into a new world of revelation. You will rise into a greater understanding of who you are in Him. This is your season to rise, and until you do, you will never see the greatest plans God had in mind concerning you.

> **YOU MUST RISE FROM THE ASHES OF YOUR PROBLEM, AND RUN HEADFIRST INTO THE SAFETY OF GOD'S SOLUTIONS.**

Forgive yourself, forgive those who tried to break you, forgive those who never showed up to help you—and rise! Your reward is waiting on you! But in order to receive it, you must rise from the ashes of your problem, and run headfirst into the safety of God's solutions. The fire will not burn you up because the Firefighter of life is standing above your head. He's extinguishing your every flame and throwing water on every spark. As flames from a fire grow and spread, it's time for you to do the same. Rise above the ashes, grow in the grace of God and receive your reward because you are *Fit to Endure the Fire!!*

About the Author

PASTOR DARRYL L. HILL

A man with an anointing on his life and a vision for leading a nation to deliverance; Pastor Darryl L. Hill is a local Pastor with a global mission, to empower and educate the nation through the Word of God. He is anointed and ordained to reach the broken-hearted, heal the sick and transform lives.

A native of Brooklyn, New York, raised in Van Dyke Projects. After traveling from state to state ministering the Word of God with Powerful Praise Crusade Ministries, Pastor Hill began pastoring in 1999. He is the founder and Senior Pastor of Powerful Praise Tabernacle in Brooklyn, New York, where the motto is "There's No Praise Like a Powerful Praise!" Since becoming Pastor, he has had an immeasurable impact on the spiritual life and growth of his congregation and community as a whole. He continues to travel across the United States, captivating the attention of many and spreading the gospel of Jesus Christ. His vision for the body of Christ is to grow collectively, and unify for the cause of Christ.

Pastor Hill has other products available. To obtain these products or to request him for a speaking engagement, please write to;

Pastor Darryl L. Hill
2140 Bergen Street
Brooklyn, NY 11233
dlhbookings@powerfulpraise.org

Or you may visit us at www.powerfulpraise.org.